DRIFT

"In a *dérive*, one or more persons during a certain period drop their relations, their work and leisure activities, and all their other usual motives for movement and action, and let themselves be drawn by the attractions of the terrain and the encounters they find there."
— Guy Debord, *Theory of the Dérive*, 1958.

The translation of *dérive* is *drift*.

LONDON

06
Masthead

07
Welcome

158
Appendix

08
How London Met Coffee
Peter Richman

22
Setting the Stage
Jacqueline Larkin

26
The Rise of Coffee in a Kingdom of Tea
Austin Langlois

34
A Head Full of Biscuits
Jonathan Shipley

36
Coffee Fit For A Queen
Nicholas O'Hara-Boyd

40
Momentum
Austin Langlois

44
(E)quality First
Brigid Quirke

52
In Good Company
Dale Arden Chong

58
City of Stimulation
Alice Hall

70
Bridging the Gap
John Surico

78
Our London
Laura Steiner

88
London Potters
John Moore

96
Pop Up Today, Gone Tomorrow
Roddy Clarke

100
Market Life
John Moore

110
Master of Reinvention
Andy Greeves

118
An Unexpected Luxury
Adam Goldberg & Daniela Velasco

128
Common Ground
Melanie Marti

146
One at a Time
Adam Goldberg

ADAM GOLDBERG
Editor in Chief

DANIELA VELASCO
Creative Director

ELYSSA GOLDBERG
Executive Editor

BONJWING LEE
Copy Editor

CONTRIBUTORS
Adam Sherrett
Alex Fleming
Alice Hall
Andy Greeves
Austin Langlois
Brigid Quirke
Dale Arden Chong
Fabian Schmid
Jacqueline Larkin
Jonathan Shipley
John Moore
John Surico
Laura Steiner
Lucia Amaddeo
Mariana Cárdenas
Melanie Marti
Nicholas O'Hara-Boyd
Peter Richman
Rapha Zurita
Roddy Clarke
Ste Murray

TO OUR READERS

For many English growing up, the clock stopped at 4 p.m. for adults: out came the fine porcelain, buttery shortbread cookies, intricately laced linens, and dark Ceylon tea. Today, a walk through London's Shoreditch or Soho neighborhoods suggests otherwise. On a rainy afternoon, young Londoners sit in small, modern coffee shops, working at their laptops drinking cup after cup of hot, brewed coffee. In the early morning, white paper cups float down Oxford Street as locals scurry to work drinking steaming-hot black coffee. Over the past 20 years, London's youth have embraced coffee as the caffeinated beverage of choice.

How is it that a country once known for its tea has become known for its diverse coffee culture? After the global financial crisis of 2008, shuttered storefronts made way for small, independent coffee shops with outlets and WiFi, serving as home-away-from home workplaces for displaced freelancers surviving in the gig economy. Immigrants from Melbourne, New York, and Tokyo opened local businesses, bringing with them elegant latte art, pour overs, and flat whites. Local roasters emerged to meet this demand, amplifying the impact of homegrown coffee culture in London. And, now, the city's booming coffee scene braces for Brexit.

In *Drift*, Volume 8: London we explore what makes London's coffee scene tick. From high coffee fit for a queen in Mayfair to everyday biscuits and markets in Shoreditch, this issue zooms in on London's coffee scene—past, present, and future—through the lens of locals and expats alike. As such, we've elected to let the writing bounce between British- and American-English so that our contributors' voices can be heard as they are.

Adam Goldberg,
Editor in Chief

How London Met Coffee

WORDS Peter Richman
PHOTOGRAPHS Rapha Zurita

Visit any specialty coffee shop and you'll find baristas describing the origin, varietal, and terroir of their pour overs. These data points are not just highbrow signals to coffee critics and connoisseurs; they enrich the experience with a pleasure beyond what's in the cup. The sweets are a little sweeter when you know the beans are Kenyan; the acidity a little brighter when you learn the altitude of the farm. In London, there's yet another data point to complement your coffee that is just as gratifying as any tasting note: the history of the London coffee shop itself.

The chronology of London's coffee shops stretches back, past the espresso boom of the 1950s, through the tea-dominant 1800s, and all the way to the mid-17th century. The city's early coffeehouses are almost always identified with the Enlightenment, the period of roughly 150 years when Europe emerged from the sluggish Middle Ages to embrace reason, progress, and critical thought. As new ideas about living and being flourished, Europeans looked beyond the church with its religion and the tavern with its ale to find a new kind of space to cultivate the mind. At the same time, a little, dark bean was slowly finding its way out of the Middle East and onto ships headed for the Mediterranean Sea. By the time this unfamiliar cargo reached the capitals of Europe, these cities were on the cusp of a new identity, brimming with kinetic energy and looking for change.

This crossing of historical paths—when Europe found coffee and coffee found Europe—was a moment of true serendipity. Coffeehouses provided the space, and coffee provided the stimulation, as Europeans furiously thought their way through the Enlightenment. They challenged authority, redefined science, and literally altered the course of Western civilization from the comfort of these coffeehouses. While the Enlightenment as an epoch defies a single cause or beginning, at its core, it relied on the rise of a public sphere where private individuals could express themselves and encounter new ideas. And while there were a variety of public spheres spread across Europe in this era, none was livelier or more influential than the 17th-century London coffeehouse.

*

It all began with an immigrant from Smyrna (or Izmir on Turkey's Aegean coast) named Pasqua Rosee. In 1652, Rosee opened London's first coffeehouse in the churchyard of St. Michael in Cornhill. Today, if

> HERE STOOD
> THE FIRST LONDON
> COFFEE HOUSE
> AT THE SIGN OF
> PASQUA ROSEE'S HEAD
> 1652

you walk south on St. Michael's Alley past the neo-Gothic church, you'll find the Jamaica Wine House on the site of Rosee's old shop, which, at the time, was really more of a stall.

By all accounts, Rosee's coffee had the flavor profile of burnt mud. The typical brewing technique of the day involved boiling and re-boiling stale grounds. But Londoners had yet to develop discerning palates, and people came from all over the city to sample the invigorating brew.

Coffeehouses had thrived across the Middle East for over a century before arriving in Western Europe. But when Rosee opened his shop, most of London still viewed coffee as a strange and exotic commodity. A savvy marketer, Rosee capitalized on this image by designing his signage with no name, just a profile of his head adorned in a turban with a twirly mustache. Before long, people nicknamed his shop The Turk's Head.

Rosee's business acumen extended well beyond branding. To drum up his customer base, he published a pamphlet titled "The Vertue of the COFFEE Drink" declaring coffee to be, among other things, "good against the Head-ache" and a "most excellent remedy against the Spleen." While his coffee was hardly the panacea Rosee advertised, the drink did in fact play a vital role in the health and wellness of many Londoners. London was a booze-soaked city at the time, in no small part because clean water was hard to come by. As a result, many people spent their days drunk—surely some by choice, but many others by necessity. Rosee's coffee offered a sobering alternative, and it was an instant hit. Seemingly overnight, Rosee was selling 600 cups a day and London was hooked on the new, energizing drink.

*

By the 1660s, coffeehouses were firmly rooted in London society. While the menus were limited, with most establishments serving some combination of coffee, tea, chocolate, and sherbet, they catered to a wide variety of cultural tastes. While Don Saltero's was a haunt for scientists, stockbrokers headed to Jonathan's, and writers frequented Button's. In contrast to the filth of the streets and foolery of the taverns, coffeehouses provided a place of relative dignity where Londoners could discuss local news and foreign affairs, business dealings and political intrigue.

In the midst of this action was Samuel Pepys, the son of a tailor who would become a member of Parliament, Secretary of the Royal Navy, and one of the finest diarists of all time. Pepys's diary, which he maintained diligently from 1660 to 1669, captures London in a remarkably tumultuous decade. Just as the country was recovering from the English Civil War, the Great Plague of London killed approximately 100,000 people in 1665. A year later, the Great Fire of London decimated the city, burning through Central London and destroying the vast majority of the city's homes. Yet through it all, despite political instability, fear of illness, and extraordinary loss of property, Londoners kept flocking to coffeehouses. If his diary is any indication, few Londoners spent more time in the city's coffeehouses than Mr. Pepys.

Pepys's diary describes his daily (and often more-than-daily) coffeehouse routine with a commitment to detail, offering an unparalleled record of coffee culture in 17th century London. We discover the coffeehouse's place in London society as he recounts the "witty and pleasant discourse" of Jon Dryden and a group of other poets. We learn about coffee's role in spreading ideas and culture, as Pepys reported that he regretted stopping at a coffeehouse to buy a book "not worth a turd." (At the time, access to printed material was a relatively new phenomenon.) More than once, Pepys recalls afternoon meetings over coffee to review the nuts and bolts of naval administration. In each of these episodes, the coffeehouse provided an alternative to the home or office—a place equally suitable for social, intellectual, and professional

pursuits. It's not hard to imagine Pepys flitting around Central London today with a laptop and leather-bound notebook, camping out in coffee shops and asking baristas for the WiFi password.

In one of his more memorable entries, Pepys writes of taking his wife to see a "ridiculous, insipid" play called "The Coffee House" in 1666. While we can only guess what theatrical mishaps warranted his harsh criticism, the mere production of the play was a statement all on its own. In less than 15 years, coffeehouses had so thoroughly permeated London culture that they were being dramatized and recreated on stage. And this perspective is what truly makes the diary an astonishing read. In Pepys's London, visiting a coffeehouse was as routine as eating supper, yet Londoners had only tasted their first sip a few years prior. In fact, coffeehouses had become accessible and affordable in a short amount of time; that they were not only fully integrated into daily life, but were well on their way to transforming London society.

*

In 1675, in a noble effort to defend "the Peace and Quiet of the Realm," King Charles II issued a proclamation outlawing all coffeehouses in England. Even at the time, the ban was an obvious political miscalculation. And while it was ultimately withdrawn before taking effect, the most controversial executive order of the day was actually the culmination of years of effort.

Although he was a fairly popular king, Charles II was a nervous ruler who worried constantly about political opposition. Understandably so, as adversaries of the Crown executed his father in 1649 and forced Charles II into exile as a teen. At age 30, he returned to London for his coronation, but the trauma of his early years left him with a deep apprehension towards political foes. In the thick of this tension, the King set his sights on coffee.

While today, the politics of coffee are mostly focused on ethical and sustainable consumption, in 17th-century England, coffee was a far more partisan affair. England's central political battle of the era, which propelled the English Civil War and continued for decades thereafter, was the power struggle between the monarchy and the Parliament. And while the Royalists assembled in the palaces, gardens, and offices of the establishment, the upstart parliamentarians (who came to be known as the Whigs) met wherever they could, whether in taverns, bookshops, or most frequently, coffeehouses. Before long, the coffeehouse was practically synonymous with political agitation.

In the years leading up to the ban, there were steady efforts to diminish the appeal of coffeehouses, which in Charles II's words promoted the "Spreading of False news." The King imposed taxes and regulations on coffeehouses and consulted with his judges on the limits of his power to attack them. Meanwhile, the Royalists stationed spies in coffeehouses throughout the country and anonymously spread pamphlets warning of a "pernicious and destructive" coffeehouse culture. None of these efforts, however, was quite as absurd or memorable as the Women's Petition Against Coffee of 1674.

According to historian Steve Pincus, it's highly unlikely that the petition was written by women. (Go ahead and read it; it's hard not to reach the same conclusion.) It may have been penned by tavern-keepers looking to nudge the public back to alcohol. But given the timing, and the lengthy attacks on coffee's "production of a thousand Monster Opinions," it was far more likely published by Charles's allies.

The petition's main thesis, that coffee left men "Eunecht" and "Impotent" and should therefore be banned, cast the women of London as a poetic pack of foul-mouthed sex addicts. And while the

petition provoked a response in the form of "The Men's Answer to the Women's Petition Against Coffee," it did little to curb the popularity of London's coffeehouses. Just a few months after the publication, the King announced his ban with an effective date of January 10, 1676. By January 8, the decree was rescinded amid overwhelming public opposition (including from some members of the King's court).

King Charles II wasn't the first leader to make this mistake. In 1511, the governor of Mecca banned coffee in an effort to thwart political dissent. When the Sultan learned of this, he declared coffee to be sacred and ordered the governor executed. While King Charles II escaped his blunder with his life, the failed effort was resounding evidence of the political will, financial support, and popular demand that 25 years of coffee had generated in London and across the U.K.

*

In 1691, a shrewd coffee entrepreneur named Edward Lloyd relocated his shop from the now-gone Tower Street to 16 Lombard Street in the heart of the city's financial district. While the prestigious new address was a clear symbol of his success, the ambitious Mr. Lloyd could have never predicted that his coffeehouse would one day become Lloyd's of London, the multi-billion pound company that dominates London's insurance market.

A few years earlier, Lloyd arrived in London with his wife and two children and opened his eponymous coffeehouse in the shadow of the Tower of London. Before long, he was serving the captains, merchants, and shipping financiers that wandered over from the docks at the nearby River Thames. Lloyd quickly gathered that his customers came for more than just coffee and sherbet; they were hungry for information, and Lloyd worked diligently to provide it. He forged a network of contacts in ports around Europe and self-published an industry newsletter with intelligence on vessels, cargo, and foreign affairs. His tables were always stocked with pens and paper and his shop soon developed a reputation as the de facto hub of maritime gossip.

As London's shipping industry grew, the demand for ship and cargo insurance grew as well, and Lloyd's Coffeehouse was the natural meeting place for buyers and sellers looking to strike a deal. More than 300 years later, while Lloyd's of London has grown into a global insurance powerhouse, it's core business of connecting brokers and underwriters is unchanged from its coffeehouse origins.

As impressive as Lloyd's story is, what's even more remarkable is that it's not unique. Sotheby's, Christie's, The Guardian, The Spectator, The Royal Exchange—each traces its roots to or through London's coffeehouses of the 17th and 18th centuries. In light of this shared lineage, it's hardly surprising that each of these businesses traffics in information. London's early coffeehouses created a new type of venue in which enterprising Londoners could transmit information by brokering, reporting, trading, and auctioneering. The lasting success of these institutions is not just a testament to the value of that information; it also affirms the power of the coffeehouses in enabling the transmission.

*

There may be no better story to capture the spirit of London' first coffeehouses than that of Sir Isaac Newton and the dolphin. Newton, the tale goes, marched into the Grecian Coffee House in Devereux Court, swept a table clear of cups and saucers, and dissected a dolphin for all to see.

Unfortunately, the story is not quite accurate. In actuality, Newton merely observed, along with astronomer Edmund Halley, while Dr. James Douglas, an anatomist who practiced midwifery, dissected the animal caught in the River Thames. And to dampen the legend even further, Dr. Douglas almost certainly performed the dissection across the street at the Royal Society, then retired to the Grecian to discuss the experiment over coffee and tobacco.

And yet, the Newtonian version of this story persists to this day, with countless histories of London's early coffeehouses invoking readers to imagine themselves walking into a coffee shop, ordering a flat white, and watching a world-famous scientist dissect a dolphin on the communal table. Perhaps the legend has survived solely for its sensationalism, but perhaps there's something more. The Newton version of the story conveys the dynamic origins of London's coffeehouses in an instant. It captures what many of us long for in a coffee shop today—a spot to gather with friends and meet interesting strangers, a place to warm our spirits while feeding our minds. But, as with the legend of Newton, when you peel back the lore and zoom in from the sweeping history of the Enlightenment past the church spires and down to the streets of London, you find a history that's more honest, more relatable, and by far more compelling. You find immigrants and entrepreneurs, books not "worth a turd," and royalty with childhood trauma. In short, you find a city full of people who just happened to be in the right place at the right time with the right bean to change history.

—

Setting the Stage

WORDS Jacqueline Larkin
ILLUSTRATION Lucia Amaddeo

During the 1950s, London became the epicentre of an espresso bar boom. Within a few years, the city was replete with hip venues serving up cups of steaming coffee. London's coffeehouse craze set a collective stage for an emerging public consciousness; so much so, that in 1954, *Architectural Design* proclaimed the presence of these progressive venues as "the greatest social revolution since the launderette." In the intimate and edgy quarters of London's espresso bars, a burgeoning generation of countercultural enthusiasts and youthful visionaries gathered to engage in political debate, recite beatnik poetry, listen to music, jive dance, lounge, smoke, and sip on frothy cappuccinos. Coffeehouses provided a progressive platform for artists to perform before a captive audience, including musicians, who began to experiment with a rebellious new genre of music: rock and roll.

The espresso revolution in England was launched by an unlikely trailblazer: a traveling dental equipment salesman from Italy named Pino Riservato. In 1951, while in London on business, Riservato became appalled with the abysmal state of the country's coffee. In the predominantly tea-drinking nation, real ground coffee was rare; many English opted instead for a substitute blend of coffee essence and chicory—a comparatively bland mixture that was served from large urns and left to sit for hours.

Riservato committed himself to the task of revolutionizing the nation's coffee culture and began marketing the Gaggia to prospective buyers: a state-of-the-art, Italian-engineered espresso machine. The entrepreneurial potential of this revolutionary mechanism was not immediately recognized. Unable to successfully market the machine to prospective buyers, Riservato chose to open his own shop as a strategic platform to showcase firsthand the Gaggia's allure. In 1952, Riservato debuted London's first espresso bar in the war-ravaged quarters of Soho, converting a bomb-damaged launderette into a business. Riservato commissioned architect Geoffrey Crockett to modernize the location's derelict interior with contemporary features including linoleum flooring, 2 and a Formica-topped bar which was crowned by the *pièce de résistance*: a glistening, gold-toned Gaggia espresso machine. Later named the Moka Bar, the atmospheric hiss, tempting aromas, and gleaming

sophistication of the location's exotic coffee apparatus captivated a cosmopolitan clientele and triggered the advent of London's espresso bar boom.

By 1960, England's coffeehouse culture had flourished, with an estimated 500 locations in the Greater London area—the vast majority situated in Soho. The informal and unconventional atmosphere of these coffeehouses deviated from the stuffy propriety of more traditional clubhouses and appealed to a strikingly diverse patronage comprised of poets, activists, academics, actors, artists, musicians, journalists, and writers. Coffeehouses were the avant-garde enclaves of a maverick society. They provided a new social space where barriers of class, gender, and race gradually dissolved. In the reclusive quarters of London's coffee bars, a generation of teens cultivated a distinctive set of beliefs that had not been possible under the austere measures of wartime society.

London became replete with coffee bars slinging cups of espresso. According to the 1959 documentary *Look At The Life*, "For every three coffee bars that opened up, two closed down." A saturated market meant business owners needed to distinguish themselves from their competitors. In an effort to do so, coffeehouse owners began to diversify, incorporating food and music into their daily offerings. Tapping into a burgeoning live music movement, managers began to feature resident bands or "skiffle groups." A style of music with jazz, blues, and folk antecedents, the skiffle genre was a precursor to rock and roll, which arguably played an important part in the early careers of many leading British musicians of the day. Coffeehouses transformed into popular, crowded nightspots where a frothy cappuccino was punctuated by a lively skiffle break. It was not uncommon for performing musicians to be paid in unlimited cups of coffee and bottles of Coca-Cola. These bands were comprised largely of amateur instrumentalists who fashioned washboards and tea chests into improvised forms of bass and percussion. It was a critical stepping stone to the second British folk revival, the blues boom, and the subsequent British invasion of the United States popular music scene.

Le Macabre, originally located at 23 Meard Street, was one such haven frequented by youthful espresso enthusiasts. To heighten its dark, underground appeal—a bohemian coffee bar with a speakeasy aesthetic—Le Macabre adopted the peculiar slogan: "Your coffee on a coffin." A 1958 film segment from the television series *British Pathé* titled "The Age Of The Teenager" featured the interior of Le Macabre. The venue channeled a morose, provocative vibe. Dim candlelight illuminated a cavernous space draped in faux cobwebs, its walls were decorated with frescoes of skeletons dancing next to nude women. Pompadoured hipsters wearing sunglasses and seated on coffins sipped cups of steaming espresso and tipped ash from their cigarettes into skulls, while a live skiffle group played a leisurely number in the background. The footage cut to one of its patrons, a bold-faced teenager who declared defiantly into the camera: "This is us, see. We're today. If you don't dig us, shoo away to some square joint with the rest of the creeps. Or why not stick around and get with it?"

Another resoundingly popular venue was the 2i's Coffee Bar, originally situated at 59 Old Compton Street, which came under the management of business partners Paul Lincoln and Ray Hunter in 1956. Long hailed as the birthplace of rock and roll in Europe, the 2i's played a formative role in the emergence of Britain's pop music culture, with multiple major acts making their debut performance in the makeshift digs of the coffeehouse's basement. The upstairs, which functioned as a coffee bar, held standing room to accommodate 25 people. A narrow stairway led down to a musty cellar, which functioned as the live music area. The "main" stage was a narrow ledge only 18 inches deep—its rough-and-ready frame comprised of milk crates and planks. A single microphone, several wall-mounted speakers, and the weak glow of exposed lightbulbs rounded out the space's crude appearance.

Live music shows were regularly packed, with audience members standing shoulder to shoulder, craning their necks to see the headlining bands performing mere feet away. During the summer, the muggy cellar became unbearably hot, prompting management to open the delivery hatch doors to the street above, releasing waves of heat, sweat, and wailing vocals. Wally Whyton, the lead vocalist and guitarist of the Vipers, one of the 2i's resident skiffle bands, described the escalating popularity of the venue, which eventually eclipsed its capacity. "The Coffee Bar simply couldn't contain the droves of people who wanted to see where it was all happening—it was only about 30 feet by 10 feet—so Paul very shrewdly opened a 2i's Club around the corner in Gerrard Street…and that's where the next wave started." The new 2i's accommodated a larger audience of rebellious youths, fueling a desire to incorporate more dynamic acts into its bill, including fledgling rock-and-rollers.

From an evolving skiffle craze emerged grassroot rock-and-rollers, including Wee Willie Harris and Tommy Steele, also referred to as the "British Elvis." Many major artists debuted at the 2i's, with the likes of Cliff Richard, Vince Eager, Tony Sheridan, Hank Marvin, Vince Taylor, and founding members of the band the Shadows being featured early in their careers on the venue's provisional stage. The 2i's surged with youth-fuelled energy, and for a time, garnered an uncontested reputation as England's most famous music spot—a status that propelled London to the frontlines of Europe's burgeoning rock scene.

Soon the Soho district became ubiquitous with cutting-edge musicians. Talent scouts, record producers, and music promoters frequented shows at the 2i's and neighboring coffeehouses, including The Cat's Whisker situated at 1 Kingly Street, in hopes of discovering new talent. Rock and roll was a controversial style of music exuding sexuality, rebelliousness, and other sentiments untoward in restrained patriarchal society. Largely banned by TV and radio stations, it was a genre almost exclusively played during BBC Radio 1's segments. Rather than hinder public interest, restricted airtime and censorship only galvanized an insatiable appetite for more. London's coffeehouses played a central role in promoting nascent rock and roll musicians by providing a platform for homegrown acts to perform, cultivate their sound, and establish a loyal following. England began producing performers the caliber of which were unprecedented, molding a generation of musicians who would usher in the British Invasion of the 1960s.

By the mid-1960s, evolving tastes resulted in a shifting patronage. The increasing popularity of discothèques, bars, and nightclubs in London coupled with the Soho's gradual gentrification made coffeehouses less relevant and increasingly *passé*. However, the ambitions of London's coffee culture have transcended social and cultural barriers to help forge a new, distinctive space of this emerging generation. As a result, Europe's rock and roll origins are deeply embedded in the intimate quarters of a dimly lit coffee bar, where a steaming espresso was served with a visceral guitar riff.

Nearly six decades after the 2i's permanently closed, a new wave of coffee shops now lines the maze-like streets of Soho's notably more commercialized quarters, signalling the next evolution of businesses serving up artisanal brews. Although a swinging skiffle group may not headline in their basement digs, London's prevailingly influential and vibrant music scene is a testament to the enduring legacy of Soho's coffeehouses. This is further evidenced by the commemorative green plaque that was unveiled in 2006 at the site of the original 2i's Coffee Bar, honouring its existence and celebrating 50 years of British rock and roll. A fitting tribute—after all, as Ringo Starr casually mentions in the tune "Rory and the Hurricanes:" "The 2i's Coffee Bar—that's where Tommy Steele would play."

—

The Rise of Coffee in a Kingdom of Tea

WORDS Austin Langlois
PHOTOGRAPHS Adam Goldberg, Daniela Velasco

The vast array of craft coffee shops across London may be surprising for those expecting to see more of the country's stereotypical beverage: tea.

While coffee and tea both arrived in England around the same time during the 17th century, tea quickly overtook its bitter sister beverage, in part due to its use as a popular medicinal drink (supposedly a cure for everything from indigestion to scurvy).

London's first coffeehouse, Pasqua Roseé, opened in the mid-1600s, and within 10 years, more than 80 coffeehouses dotted the city. But, tea was seen as a luxury (as it was more expensive than coffee) and became a drink for the wealthy and the royals—a high-class commodity. As such, tea was more popular and more desirable than coffee until the late 20th century.

However, in recent years, tea consumption has begun to decline while coffee consumption continues to rise. Data from the U.K. Department for Environment, Food, and Rural Affairs show a 63 percent decrease in tea consumption from 1974 to 2014—a stark contrast to the tripling of coffee consumption within the same timeframe.

An article in *The Atlantic* suggests the decline of tea could be due to the drink's connection with biscuits, cakes, and other sweets, which have also "fallen out of favor as new data shows British consumers have tried to move away from sugar and bread toward healthier trends."

Another reason for tea's decline may be the shift from black brews to herbal and fruity blends. U.K. magazine *The Grocer* reported earlier this year that British retail giant Tesco dropped about 40 percent of its SKUs from tea manufacturer Tetley, "as the retailer opted for trendier fruity and herbal lines."

And while there are many factors at play with the decline in tea drinking across the U.K., the decline seems to correlate with the increase in

Will Homer, Prufrock Coffee

Alek Smet, Workshop Coffee

coffee consumption, a trend that accelerated since the start of the millennium.

Second wave coffee culture (led by early specialty coffee companies such as Starbucks and Peet's) expanded across the United States as early as the 1960s. But it wasn't until the 1990s that second wave hit Britain in full force, and the 2000s when artisanal, thoughtfully sourced coffee became popular that British coffee culture began to brew.

Many attribute the boom to James Hoffman and Anette Moldvaer of Square Mile Coffee Roasters, two of the pioneers of the specialty coffee scene in London. Together, they founded their coffee company, an award-winning roaster that sells primarily wholesale to more than 150 bars, cafes, and restaurants worldwide.

"Tea is a really an in-home beverage. No one buys cups of tea outside of the home or in cafes—or certainly not many do," said Hoffman. "Coffee replaced beer as the out-of-the-home, socializing beverage. The trend of cafes opening has neatly coincided with massive numbers of pubs closing—a trend that only seems to continue."

The trend Hoffman mentioned is in reference to Allegra Group's recent research, which shows that coffee shops are forecasted to overtake pubs by 2030. In early 2018, Allegra released its Project Café 2018 U.K. Report, which showed a 5.4 percent growth in coffee shops. The total clocked in at 24,061 cafes—a substantial increase from the 80 in the 1600s.

But coffee's integration into the British beverage culture hasn't been completely smooth. Marco Arrigo of Bar Termini said he saw a bit of resistance from the current coffee industry.

"[Initially,] purveyors of Italian coffee blends in the U.K. and specialty coffee producers had trouble understanding each other. I was guilty of that too. [Disagreement] was primarily around the style of the roasts and the fruity or green notes found within the coffee."

However, as the demand for coffee continued to grow, both factions of coffee producers found there were plenty of customers to go around.

"At a consumer level, the prevalence of new specialty coffee bars now is proof that whatever resistance may have existed is no longer there, and quality coffee in all its forms is capturing consumer imagination."

Instead, Arrigo said, the challenge now is to make enough money, as the cost of living in London continues to soar.

"Unfortunately, serving tea and coffee alone can mean struggling to pay the high rents of Central London. Our Bar Termini is an Italian bar concept that served coffee in the mornings and cocktails all night. Cafes in London will be moving towards alcohol, so they can work the bar from morning to night to pay their bills."

While tea is also still very much a celebrated beverage—and promoted to tourists as part of the quintessential British experience (e.g., afternoon tea)—it is now more commonly enjoyed at home, while coffee is the see-and-be-seen drink of choice.

"Tea has long been seen as the national drink in the U.K. To some people, it is more than a drink, actually; it is almost a way of life," said food and beverage operations manager Agnieszka Josko of boutique hotel Flemings Mayfair.

But, if the numbers are any indication, coffee may soon be a way of life, too.

—

A Head Full of Biscuits

WORDS Jonathan Shipley
ILLUSTRATIONS Mariana Cárdenas

Before Mary, Queen of Scots lost her head, she often filled her head with a good biscuit. She loved a buttery shortbread at court and ate them prodigiously. She particularly liked the shortbread flavored with caraway seeds, or the thin, buttery-sweet treat known as the petticoat tail.

Cooks at the Scottish royal court were creating the dainty petticoat tails, along with rounds and fingers, for the queen. Some claim that the name was a corruption of *petites galettes*, or "little cakes" in French (after all, Mary's mother was French, and, in addition to being Queen of the Scots, she was also, briefly, Queen of France); others say that the shortbread triangles were shaped like the petticoats of court ladies at the time. The first shortbreads were served at only very special occasions, such as weddings, Christmas, and on New Year's Eve. Serving them showed off one's wealth as only the upper class could afford butter, sugar, and flour.

Although Mary lost her head before Scotland was united with England, the love affair with the biscuit endures among the British of today. Biscuits—a category including fig rolls, shortcakes, the Garibaldi, the Duchy, the Finger Cream, the Bourbon, the Rich Tea Finger, and more—are as synonymous with London as is fog.

According to the Oxford English Dictionary, by definition, a biscuit is "a small, baked, and unleavened cake, typically crisp, flat, and sweet." Latin for "twice-cooked," it was, in its earliest iterations, a paste of flour and water, spread thin and baked.

Many trace the biscuit, or cookie, to ancient Persia. By the 7th century, cooks in the Persian Empire were making bread-based mixtures, sweetening them with cream, fruit, and honey. One of the earliest spiced biscuits was gingerbread. When the Persians invaded Europe, they brought with them both the food they made, and the ingredients to make them—most notably spices that would become an important global commodity. As a result, cookies began to make inroads in the West.

Soon, they were present at some of Europe's most important historical events. In the 1100s, King Richard I of England brought biscuits with him on the Third Crusade. Swedish nuns were making gingerbread in the 14th century. By the 16th century, ginger biscuits were being sold in town squares throughout Europe to ease citizens' digestion. By the 1850s, there were British biscuit firms throughout the country—early ones including McVities (still a major snack food brand offering biscuits that include digestives, fig rolls, and ginger nuts), Carr's (now part of United Biscuits, a multinational food manufacturer listed on the London Stock Exchange), and Crawford's (also owned by United Biscuits, Crawford's makes shortbreads and other snacks).

As the Industrial Revolution gained full steam, and the biscuit business, in turn, became industrialized, so did cookie docking (perforating the dough with small holes to prevent the dough from blowing up with steam during the baking process) and decoration. T&T Vicars Biscuit Machinery & General Engineers, established in 1849 and still in operation, has always looked for new ways to improve the biscuit making process. With advances in machinery, the company and its competitors began making biscuits distinctive, by color, by shape, and by embossing them in specific ways. Take, for instance, Oreo cookies—an American cookie with European roots. It is said that the cookie's emboss, a variation of the Nabisco logo, is either an early European symbol for quality or a Cross of Lorraine, which was carried by the Knights Templar into the Crusades. Rich Tea and Morning Coffee biscuits are still being made in much the same way that they were a hundred-plus years ago. There are still Victorian ferns adorning the Custard Cream (first created in 1908) and on the aforementioned Morning Coffee biscuit is the Art Deco design of a cup of tea.

Today, there are Jammie Dodgers (shortbread biscuits filled with raspberry or strawberry jam) and Custard Creams (cookie sandwich biscuits filled with custard cream), digestives (semi-sweet meal biscuits) and Hobnobs (commercial, rolled oat biscuits). And when there are no biscuits to be had, it can be a national calamity. In 2017, there was a flood in the city of Carlisle, home to one of the nation's largest producers of ginger biscuits and Bourbons (a dark chocolate sandwich cookie with a chocolate buttercream filling). The flood not only crippled the company, but the British love of biscuits. Relief arrived when two Boeing 777s filled with biscuits arrived in England from the United Arab Emirates.

Today, chocolate digestive biscuits are exceedingly popular amongst Londoners. So are the aforementioned Jammie Dodgers, Custard Creams, and Jaffa Cakes. McVitie's brand of biscuits sells like mad. So does Lotus Biscoff and Crawford's. Though high tea is mostly a tourist thing, Londoners have a cup of tea and some biscuits on a 10-minute break in the afternoon, still, as always.

From a Persian cook thousands of years ago, in a palace thousands of miles away, to a man eating Jammie Dodgers on a train during his evening commute, the biscuit has endured. From a medieval nun creating digestive aids to school kids eating Jaffa Cakes. From Mary, Queen of Scots eating caraway seed cookies to a dock worker from Lewisham eating a Rich Tea Finger, it's a sweetness that's helped define the British to a T.
—

MANY THANKS FOR YOUR FEEDBACK!

For the 2018 calendar year, we have added for the first time a new layout combined with a new corporate typeface, Sweet Sans. Our goal was to create a more clear and reserved layout while maintaining our functional details.

Your opinion was very important to us and we are happy that so many of you participated in our feedback drive. We have checked and discussed your feedback and suggestions and have incorporated much of this in the layout:

Improved orientation and readability in the calendar year

- Dates are emphasized through a bolder font.
- The month is placed at the outer page border so that you can find the date even when flipping pages quickly.

More space for entries on the weekend

- In our daily planner, Saturday and Sunday will from now on each have an individual page.
- At the same time, our weekly planner in Medium and Master formats will include an individual column for Saturday and Sunday.

Planning down to the last detail

- The year overview will from now on include the entire following year.

We naturally look forward to your further ideas and suggestions on how we can make our products even better: service@leuchtturm1917.de

We thank you for your loyalty and wish you lots of enjoyment with your new LEUCHTTURM1917 planner!

KURT STURKEN   AXEL STURKEN   MAX STURKEN

BITTE BENUTZEN SIE DIESE ETIKETTEN ZUR BESCHRIFTUNG DER TITEL UND RÜCKEN IHRES **LEUCHTTURM1917** BUCHES, WENN SIE ES ARCHIVIEREN MÖCHTEN.
PLEASE USE THIS STICKERS FOR LABELLING THE TITLE AND SPINE OF YOUR **LEUCHTTURM1917** BOOK WHEN YOU WANT TO ARCHIVE IT.
VEUILLEZ UTILISER CES ETIQUETTES SUR LE TITRE ET LE DOS DE VOTRE **LEUCHTTURM1917** CARNET POUR L'IDENTIFIER AVANT DE LA RANGER.

LEUCHTTURM1917

LEUCHTTURM1917

LEUCHTTURM1917

LEUCHTTURM1917

BISCUITS

01. THE GARIBALDI
02. THE DUCHY
03. THE FINGER CREAM
04. THE BOURBON
05. THE RICH TEA FINGER
06. GINGER BISCUITS
07. OREO COOKIES
08. RICH TEA BISCUITS
09. MORNING COFFEE BISCUITS
10. CUSTARD CREAM
11. JAMMIE DODGERS
12. JAFFA CAKES
13. FIG ROLLS
14. SHORTCAKES

Coffee Fit For A Queen

WORDS Nicholas O'Hara-Boyd
PHOTOS Adam Goldberg

Ask anyone not particularly cluey on England what the country is famous for and, invariably, they're bound to list one of the following: Big Ben, the Queen, and tea. The latter has become so synonymous with English culture that you could barely be blamed for being confused at the sight of anything else being drunk after hopping off a plane at Heathrow. It therefore takes a certain degree of brazen determination to throw out the handbook and help to pioneer England's coffee culture.

H.R. Higgins was a London war veteran with humble beginnings. A grocer by trade, he started brewing his own coffee in a tiny flat in pre-WWI London. In 1942, he opened his shop selling a drink no one was particularly interested in at the time and, being unique in doing so, he become known simply as "the coffee man."

While the shop enjoyed a certain popularity in the English coffeehouses of the 17th and 18th centuries, more importantly, Higgins was among the first of his day to declare he wasn't content with the generic and homogenised beans being shipped from abroad. He, instead, yearned for what would come to be branded as single origin. He wanted to know the individual farms his beans were coming from to better appreciate, and ultimately have more control over, their product's flavour profile.

In what must have seemed a lot like an Indiana Jones adventure mission in early-1960s London, he took matters into his own hands. He chartered a small plane and flew to Kenya where, after enduring a long and tortuous bus journey to Nairobi alongside some chickens and goats, he met with the chief of the Chagga tribe. "You are our first coffee friend in London, Mr. Higgins," David told me, recounting what his grandfather, H.R., told him the Chagga chief said. "You can buy from us directly."

Nearly 60 years on, H.R. Higgins Ltd still stocks that very bean—the Tanzania Kibo Chagga—in its homey shop on the outskirts of Mayfair. Buzzing from early morning until late into the evening, its peaceful atmosphere makes for a favourite haunt among laid-back locals and busy professionals alike. All seem to be in agreement: this smooth, rich coffee is something special.

Now run by H.R.'s son Tony and grandson David, the business has stayed in the family following H.R.'s death in 1968. "We still do the

roasting ourselves," David says fondly, as he seems to do with anything regarding his family: "He's [Tony] 81 and was there for most of the day yesterday!"

David began working in the shop at age 15 and, now nearly four decades later, is still driven by a sense of legacy and passion. "I quite like the romance of it all," he says, wistfully, between sips. There certainly is something romantic about owning one of London's most iconic coffee shops in one of London's most iconic neighbourhoods. What's even more romantic still is when you're not only loved by the commoners, but also by the royals.

A Royal Warrant is just about the highest honour you can be given as a British goods or services purveyor. It is a licence issued by the sovereign indicating that the business is an official supplier to a member of the royal family. To qualify, the business must have provided services to the member on an ongoing basis for at least three years. H.R. Higgins has held a royal warrant from the Queen for 39 years.

"Basically, someone from Buckingham Palace rang, described the desired flavours, and it went from there."

What flavours does Her Majesty favour? "I could tell you but then I'd have to kill you," David chuckles. "We're not allowed to tell anyone which coffee it is."

Once a warrant is awarded, it is reviewed every five years for renewal. "It has mostly to do with ethical trading, such as the sustainability of your product and the reduction of plastics and packaging," he explains. As for its competition, it's hard to know what it's up against and, as English rules dictate, lobbying is also out of the question. "In a lot of ways, you're lucky to get it and just hope to hold onto it."

David would not tell me exactly which bean the Queen prefers. But if David's hint of a wry smile is anything to go off, smart money says the head of the Commonwealth's java bean choice is among the 31 flavours currently offered to all customers. Among them are: the 1942 Blend that pays homage to the shop's origins; the customer favourite Nicaragua La Bastilla Blueberry Candy; and Jamaica Blue Mountain, which is easily the most expensive bean at £196/kg (US$250/2.2lbs). But it's perhaps the Galapagos San Cristobal medium roast that is the company's most unique. It is sourced directly from a coffee farm on the volcanic island of San Cristobal (the famous naturalist Darwin went ashore in 1835) inside the National Park and sent to London in tiny packages—the sign of a coffee shop willing to travel to the end of the world for its customers.

Perhaps those lengths are every bit tied to H.R. Higgins's sense of duty as it is to the company's business model. "We have a lot of customers who have been with us for a very long time," David explains. "An elderly lady once told me my grandfather taught her how to make coffee as a little girl. They're a part of our lives and we're a part of theirs. It's a bit like a family."

One of London's finest qualities is the way it honours the past by preserving it for the future. H.R. Higgins, one of London's most respected coffee shops for the better part of the last century, is no different. "I think my granddad would have been chuffed to bits. His origins are so humbling; the idea of him roasting on that little machine in a shabby room is so far removed from Mayfair or royal warrants." Perhaps H.R.'s real legacy, however, was his adoring family, willing to go to whatever lengths necessary to protect his vision and see the day when London would become a coffee connoisseur's paradise, in no small part with H.R. Higgins to thank.

—

Momentum

WORDS Austin Langlois
PHOTOGRAPHS Adam Goldberg, Daniela Velasco

While London ranks fourth on the global list of cities with the most Starbucks cafes, the third-wave coffee scene has reached its own heights in London. And, if you ask around London to understand where the city's craft coffee scene began, it seems like all roads lead back to one place: Square Mile Coffee Roasters out of East London.

It doesn't have a physical storefront or cafe, but it's likely that anyone who has grabbed a cup of joe in the British capital has already tasted Square Mile's coffee. The roaster wholesales its coffee to some 150 cafes, restaurants, hotels, and shops around the world. While its footprint is primarily centered within the U.K., you'll also find its beans pop up across the globe, in places like Boutique Coffee in San Mateo, California; Menta Specialty Coffee Shop in Lefkosa, Cyprus; and Sage & Sirloin in Hamala, Bahrain.

The roastery was founded by James Hoffmann (2007 World Barista Champion) and Anette Moldvaer (a World Cup Tasting Champion) in 2008. Hoffmann's introduction to coffee was through a job demonstrating domestic espresso machines in a department store in Victoria, London; later, he started his own gig as a coffee product and business development consultant. Moldvaer started as a barista at Dromedar in Trondheim, Norway before working at the London-based Supplier Mercanta and The London School of Coffee.

"Before Square Mile, both myself and my business partner had been working in coffee education," said Hoffmann." I think there comes a point where you feel like you should stop telling people how to do it, and go out and do it yourself. It was a business that was started from a place of passion but not a great deal of business knowledge—which we've worked hard to rectify since."

And while people attribute the start of the London craft coffee scene to Square Mile, Hoffmann says it was due more to the communal nature of the city's nascent industry in the mid-2000s. "The early years were exciting, manic, and frantic but full of energy and momentum. I think London's scene boomed so well because London had built a really cohesive [coffee] community all working towards the same thing."

One example he mentioned was World Barista Champion Gwilym Davies's Disloyalty Card, a free coffee passport of sorts. Patrons who visited all eight of the East London coffee shops on the card received a free coffee at Davies's coffee shop, Prufrock.

Moldvaer and Hoffmann's legacy since then has reached beyond cafes and roasteries. Each has also each published coffee guidebooks, combining their experiences in the coffee industry as baristas and educators. Moldvaer's *Coffee Obsession*, breaks down more than 100 coffee recipes from around the globe—it's like a training handbook for non-baristas. The book dives into everything from growing and harvesting to roasting and brewing.

And you'll find Hoffmann's books in cafes across the world, from Lisbon to Bali. *The Atlas of Coffee* (its second edition was released in late 2018) dives deep into the coffee process from bean to brew. But what's most interesting is the country-by-country overview of the coffee production in more than 35 countries, detailing historical background, growing regions, coffee varieties, and more. To date, it has sold more than 200,000 copies, with an audience that encompasses both coffee newbies and experts alike.

"It was a much bigger and more difficult project than I initially imagined," said Hoffmann. "In the course of writing the book, it became clearer to me that I wanted this book to be a kind of guidebook to this new world of coffee that had seemingly come out of nowhere, and yet seemed so fully formed. I was frustrated by our reputation as an industry of being pretentious, exclusive, and snobby. I tried to write a book that made coffee more accessible and inclusive."

Out of everything he learned, he said that what surprised him the most was how brutal and, frankly, unpleasant the history of coffee production was. "I think I'd come into coffee at a time when all the messaging around sourcing had been so positive, so focused on rewarding quality, that I hadn't understood the endemic unfairness that the industry is built upon."

And it is those values of sustainable sourcing, a focus on quality and ethical business practices, with which Square Mile Coffee Roasters now not only operates but also leads the British coffee industry–and the third-wave coffee culture–by example.

—

Square Mile Coffee served at Kaffeine

(E)quality First

WORDS Brigid Quirke
PHOTOGRAPHS Adam Goldberg, Daniela Velasco

Located in a prefab WWII Nissen hut in the prestigious gallery quarter of Tate Britain, one of the Tate's four museums, the Roastery at Tate is an unexpected player in the London coffee scene. It supplies small-batch, roasted coffee to the Tate Modern cafe and its counterparts in Liverpool and St. Ives, subverting expectations of watery lattes that might usually find a home in gallery cafes. Its approach is unique—while most specialty coffee spaces in London claim quality as their paramount concern, this is not the case for the Roastery at Tate.

"Quality isn't our starting point," explains head roaster Thomas Haigh. "Equality is. That doesn't mean quality doesn't matter or that we don't produce quality coffee. But if we keep considering equality as secondary to the way coffee tastes, we aren't moving forward." Unlike many specialty roasters in London and throughout Europe, the Roastery at Tate is committed to gender equity at origin as its paramount focus.

The Gender Equity Project was launched by the roastery three years ago, promoting gender equity in the coffee sourcing process. Haigh, with the help of import and export partner companies, seeks out and visits farms that are headed by and support women producers, learns about the cost of production in the area, and deals directly with these producers, offering a fair, sustainable price for the beans that make their way to the Tate. Through this process, growers are paid at least 50 percent more than the minimum standard price set by Fairtrade Organic. In 2018, for example, the Roastery at Tate bought coffee from Gloria Esperanza Meija, a grower in Honduras, at 167 percent above the Fairtrade price.

What began as a gender-focused project has morphed, in Haigh's words, into a wider conversation about marginalization in coffee production. Three years after the project's launch, he's now also seeking to support indigenous communities and those disadvantaged by geographical poverty through the same process of buying directly for a fair, sustainable price.

Haigh realized that many of these growers lack access to the processes and resources he is familiar with: "You've got keen people producing incredible coffee. But they don't have the same access to buyers, and they're not getting any of the profit from the coffee boom here in the U.K."

A recent sourcing trip to Peru highlighted this disparity. In Chirinos, in northern San Ignacio, extensive regional investment in road infrastructure has increased producers' access to market and coffee institutions, allowing them to perfect post-harvesting techniques desirable in the specialty coffee market, and in turn, earn a good price for their product. The southern neighbouring region of Jaen, by the flip of a political coin, lacks this investment, meaning growers are not accessing the same kind of profits as their neighbours.

"Their understanding of quality and their access to resources and education [are] minimal, in comparison to the growers in the North. It's arbitrary, but there's this lack of cultural knowledge which makes coffee far less profitable for them." In Jaen, smallholding coffee producers perform their own processing and drying, as transportation is difficult without basic infrastructure. This makes it harder to preserve and enhance the quality and flavor of the coffee being produced.

This lack of access, Haigh explains, is the main focus of the Roastery at Tate's current ethos. "We talk about cup scores and defects—the growers don't understand that; they look at the health of the plants and the smell of the coffee. But the most important aspect of quality, profit-wise, is measured in terms of how it fits the Q-grading standards set by the Coffee Quality Institute." While it's important that these frameworks exist to drive innovation in specialty coffee, Haigh explains, "It can create a really narrow idea of where good coffee comes from and what it should taste like."

And so, a disparity exists between those with access to the knowledge

and technology to meet specialty coffee quality standards, and those without. The Roastery at Tate is seeking to bridge that gap, both by supporting and educating growers at origin, and by promoting a wider conversation among buyers and coffee drinkers. For Haigh, this means seeking out disadvantaged growers and working alongside companies like Falcon Specialty that provide guidance and support for these growers when it comes to meeting the quality standards that will turn a profit.

This ethos flips the status quo approach to quality. By building relationships with keen coffee producers otherwise disadvantaged through gender, geography, or demography, the Roastery at Tate can support these groups by investing time and money into farms, processes, and education, helping them to produce high-quality, profitable coffee in the long term.

The access to cultural knowledge with which the roastery is concerned doesn't exist in a vacuum—the process of demystifying the industry is pertinent at all stages of the supply chain. "Promoting equality doesn't have to cost more money. It just costs the time and thought that goes into widening your view of what's possible. If consumers begin asking questions about where that coffee comes from and who is truly affected by it, those roasters in turn will start asking questions about their importers and suppliers—it's a trickle up effect."

The Roastery at Tate sought to take this approach to the roasting equipment housed in the Nissen hut, sharing roasting knowledge and skills within the London coffee scene. To put this ethos into practice and garner a community of like-minded roasters in London, the Roastery at Tate opened the Slot Roasting Collective, a co-roasting space for coffee shops and groups who want to try their hands at roasting. By mentoring the next generation of roasters in London, the Roastery at Tate can ensure that (e)quality extends beyond its operations. This intentionality underpins much of what Haigh and the Roastery at Tate focus on—removing barriers within the industry.

"We just want our equipment to be used, and we want it to be a sustainable space. Then, you've got really great, innovative people in a room, and we're all learning together—like the things being done by Girls Who Grind Coffee (GWGC), for example."

Haigh is talking about Fi O'Brien and Casey Lalonde, who spent some time at the Roastery at Tate in 2017. The pair went on to launch GWGC, a Somerset-based small-batch roastery sourcing coffee exclusively from female growers. With an uncompromising focus on empowering women, GWGC works with female cooperatives and non-profit organisations that support women in the industry.

GWGC is succeeding in the trickle-up way Haigh talks about—Casey and Fi launched their first coffee produced by a female cooperative, ASDECAFE, at a breast cancer awareness event in London in 2017; they now produce five different single-origin coffees produced by women, to empower women.

In an industry that often operates with a one-track focus on quality that can sideline issues of equality, people like Haigh, Fi, and Casey offer a refreshing alternative. By taking a different approach to defining quality, they roast coffee that has a powerful impact at the source.

In the current political and social climate, this approach is more than just novel—it feels necessary. "I get all tingly thinking about the potential for equity here," says Haigh, "and I do feel like now is the time that change will happen."
—

Tate Roastery

In Good Company

WORDS Dale Arden Chong
PHOTOGRAPHS Daniela Velasco

While strangers commute together beneath the hum of the city on the London Tube, others cycle to their destination. Many make a stop at a the city's top-notch coffee shops for a drink before they continue on their way.

According to freelance photographer and avid cyclist Joe Harper, it's extremely rare for bicyclers to go on a ride that does not pause for coffee. "People are fiercely loyal to the coffee spots they go to," he said. "There's always one person asking, 'When's the coffee stop, how long until coffee?'" One of note, he said is Giro in Esher. Located along the Box Hills, a route known for its challenging climb that attracts many cyclists for training or personal achievement, the cafe can be described as a "nearly there" spot. Harper mentioned that the coffee shop is one of the few that people truly seek out, as well. "[The cafe is] connected with the cycling sphere and community, because it's a cycling coffee shop. It's a route everyone rides."

Though cycling is a sport that is often enjoyed independently, it is riding with others that makes the experience memorable, according to Simon Mottram, who founded Rapha, another clubhouse-coffeehouse that cyclists frequent. Despite the fact that Rapha is a cycling apparel and accessories company, the true driving force behind the brand is its ability to bring the cycling community together. "Cycling independently has many benefits, but riding together is what will keep people's interest in the sport longer," Mottram said. With Rapha's 200 weekly organized rides around the world for cyclists of all levels, and hundreds of additional rides organized both by the company as well as patrons of its members-only group Rapha Cycling Club, the brand strives to be the avenue by which enthusiasts of all backgrounds come together while cycling, and during the hours in between rides.

For Harper, it was riding with others that initially got him interested in the sport when he first moved to London. "It was a guy from Minnesota

	— GUESTS
SATURDAY	SOHO CLUBHOUSE RIDE
SUNDAY	SPITALFIELDS CLUBHOUSE R... **INTERMEDIATE**

Rapha

CAFE
EVENTS
RACE VIEWING
GROUP RIDES

who got a friend of mine into cycling, and then I bought a bike and we ended up riding together all the time," he said. In the end, it was just Harper and the Minnesota-native who would go on rides, most of which were often based on visiting multiple coffee shops. Before long, he found himself pushing further and further into the sport of road cycling.

The photographer also explained how transitioning from cycling as a recreational activity to an athletic sport, which attracted him to cycling in groups rather than by himself, changed his experience. "When you get that many people, there's always someone to ride with...there are new people who want to introduce you to more people or try new things," he said. "It's nice to have that kind of community and support network—especially if someone has an accident on the road." Harper shared the example of one of his friends, who was recently knocked off of his bike; Harper could serve as a witness for the accident. "No one wants to go out and train at 6 a.m., especially in the winter when it's raining and icy. When you have four, five, or six other people who are going to do it with you, it's so much nicer and easier."

According to Mottram, Rapha sees everyone from freelancers and designers to architects and lawyers as a part of the clubhouse community, whether they are officially Rapha club members or not. Rapha first made its mark on the cycling world in 2004 as a direct-to-consumer brand through its website Rapha.cc, where it continues to sell its own all-weather cycling clothes and accessories. Mottram's love for cycling began when he was a child, but it wasn't until he was older, during the mid-1980s, that he found a passion in professional cycling. As a result of his love for the sport, he created Rapha to tell the story of bicycling. "I became obsessed with the drama, the heroes, the characters." It wasn't until 2012 that the company opened up its first clubhouse in London. Now, the brand has two clubhouses in the city, one located in Soho and the other in East London in Old Spitalfields Market.

Of course, while rides were created to bring cyclists together, it's in the moments before or after, and occasionally those pauses in between the rides, when people truly experience the perks of being a part of a clique built around shared interests, a sentiment that led Rapha to open up brick-and-mortar locations known as clubhouses. There, cycling enthusiasts and club members can come together over a cup of coffee at the clubhouse cafe, as well as shop for more Rapha products. Morgan highlights the average routine, "On any given weekday morning, the cafe will be heaving with bikes and cyclists as many riders use it as a pit stop after their morning ride—picking up a coffee hit before they head onwards to the office," he explained.

Coffee shops such as Giro or Rotate, a newly-opened cycling cafe in Shoreditch, as well as other spots along common cycling routes, also serve as meeting spots for cyclists. "There's infrastructure at these places so you can safely keep your bike, and there are little things you can pick up—even the decoration of the place—to make you feel more comfortable," Harper said. "A lot of people don't feel comfortable going into Starbucks wearing full Lycra. You can go somewhere people aren't judged for wearing sports clothes."

Even when the cafes are not expressly inspired by cycling, they all cater to their cycling customers. Whether they are televising live races, selling nutrition bars, or providing spaces to meet before and after each ride, these coffee shops have become a natural (and arguably vital) addition for any route in London. A whole ecosystem has been built around these cyclists. According to Harper, the smartphone app Strava tracks a cyclist's route and offers a list of recommended coffee shops along the way.

For Mottram, coffee and cycling have always been linked. "From the early pros sipping espresso on their bikes to the cafe becoming a traditional gathering places pre- and post-ride. Coffee is a stimulant, socially and physiologically, which helps when you need a little extra push on a climb. The communities of cycling and coffee aren't so different from each other, either. "Like cycling, a good coffee is made better with good company."

Though each rider may have specific spots he or she prefers, each ride will, without a doubt, have a coffee break somewhere along the route, according to Harper. "Sometimes, if you're on a ride and you can't get a spot in, you have to do a massive detour or loop back around," he said. As coffee shops in London continue to create places designed to provide a space for cyclists to come together and build relationships, they're not only giving their customers a unique and specialized home away from home, they're giving them a family too.

—

City of Stimulation

WORDS Alice Hall
FILM PHOTOGRAPHS ON KODAK TRI-X 400 Fabian Schmid

Author Edward Abbey famously declared: "Our culture runs on coffee and gasoline, the first often tasting like the second."

Like T.S. Eliot's Prufrock (from *The Love Song of J. Alfred Prufrock*), who measured out his life in "coffee spoons," the lives of London residents are undoubtedly governed by the power of the sepia liquid just as much as they are by the underground transport system snaking beneath the city streets. Serving a culturally and geographically diverse 1.37 billion passengers a year, the London Underground, much like the coffee that fuels those who take it, performs the critical function of spurring the city into action. Coffee runs through the arteries of Londoners just as the Tube runs through the arteries of the city, propelling the city and the people living in it.

The coffee bean's historical origins demonstrate that its primary purpose was to stimulate. Some of the earliest accounts of drinking coffee can be traced to the Sufi tribes in Yemen, whose men sipped the liquid in order to maintain mental agility during a religious ceremony. In his book *The Coffee-House: A Cultural History*, Markman Ellis recalls how foreign visitors perceived coffee-drinkers for the first time and noted that they had "no apparent desire for sleep but with mind and body continuously alert, men talked and argued, finding in the hot black liquor a curious stimulus."

The purpose of coffee and electrical impulses can be traced to the origins of the word *stimulation*. Obtained from the Latin *stimulatus*, the word originates from the 1610s, when it was defined as "rouse to action." Stimulation is the driving energy behind movement and potential, which is the heart of all progress. Whilst the London Underground carves an external physical route to business meetings, new relationships, and old friendships, it is coffee's caffeine jolt that provides us with the internal mental route, so to speak.

Positioned at the collision point between these two aspects of the city are the owners of the small coffee carts that park outside popular underground stations. Despite an influx of commercial chains that are flooding London's streets, their business remains unaffected as they fulfill the vital duty of awakening the hoards of bleary-eyed commuters. When asked what coffee means to London, Sophie, who works on a pop-up cart outside Shoreditch Station, told me how her customers depend on it: "People use the Underground to commute to work and people rely on coffee to work. Both are what keep us connected."

All too often, Londoners find themselves dashing through the streets and hailing taxis whilst attempting to juggle a lukewarm flat white and a conference call.

Yet on occasion, the screeching electrified tracks can be a deeply unsettling and lonely sound for the commuter. Its announcements even conjure ghosts: Back in 2013, a widowed woman used to make frequent visits to Embankment Station to hear her deceased husband's voice say "Mind the gap" over the intercom recording. The over-stimulation of modern city life can have the effect of anesthetizing us—as Tube riders stare at their phones, alone, in a sea of other commuters. Perhaps the same can be said for coffee. Alongside amicable interactions, it can be the channel to break-ups, bereavements, and introspective loneliness.

It is not only the mayhem of the morning commute from which these baristas seek business. Sophie is still serving coffee outside the station as the evening begins. Both coffee and the London Underground provide us with the uniting power of home. Coffee conjures memories for everyone. For some, it may transport them back to a hometown in Yemen; for others, it's a metaphorical home, where stories are shared with relatives over a hot brew. In a city as diverse as London, home is an entirely subjective experience. It is what unites us in getting there that matters.

To use the words of Samuel Johnson, "When a man is tired of London, he is tired of life." When someone tires of consuming coffee in London, they tire of more than a grounded mahogany powder. They tire of the sparkly animation it injects into one of the world's most diverse and enchanting cities.

—

Andre Alfaro, Euston Station

Adrian Guevara, Old Street Station

Georgia Graham, Old Street Station

Pilar Quiros, Shoreditch High Street Station

Sevgi Ismailova, Shoreditch High Street Station

Bridging the Gap

WORDS John Surico
PHOTOGRAPHS Ste Murray

London often seems like an urban paradox. It has the auspices of an age-old metropolis—with its Victorian architecture, red phone booths, dim pubs, and cobblestone streets—yet something about it is incredibly modern. That dynamic works in tandem, a friction that gives London the characteristic that defines every great city: constant flux.

But, of course, the United Kingdom capital is not immune to the rapid changes that we're witnessing in cities worldwide. Since 2011, rent for a two-bedroom flat here has risen more than three times faster than wages, one alarming study recently showed. In several neighborhoods, rents jumped by as much as 30 percent. Between 2018 and 2026, the city's population will grow by a full tenth, reaching close to 10 million people. And by then, a number of huge development projects will essentially sculpt a skyline out of thin air, the most notable being the "mini-Manhattan" on London City Island.

Yet for transit and urban observers—myself included—London appears increasingly up for the challenges it faces. The city is widely recognized as one that invested smartly in its infrastructure, making key decisions to ensure that its greatest network—the Underground—and other systems would continue to grow in lockstep with the city. City officials chose to invest not only just in maintenance, but also, in building out new networks, like the Overground and DLR, to accommodate an expanding global capital. Within antiquity, the system has innovated, adding contactless payment and modern-day signals. And the city has even found a way to pay for it all: by charging drivers to enter London's busiest areas, lessening congestion and improving air quality. As a result, these systems are remarkably reliable, day in and day out.

That's what has long fascinated me about Crossrail, which is Europe's largest infrastructure project underway. When it partially opens in September of 2019, the $20 billion line will mark the most significant expansion to the London rail system in decades. The train—which will be known to most as the purple Elizabeth line—will complement the Underground and National Rail by piecing together gaps in the city's periphery, ultimately cutting commute times in half, while increasing Central London's rail capacity by an astonishing 10 percent.

Most London residents agree that Crossrail is desperately needed, especially in East London, where the population in the borough of

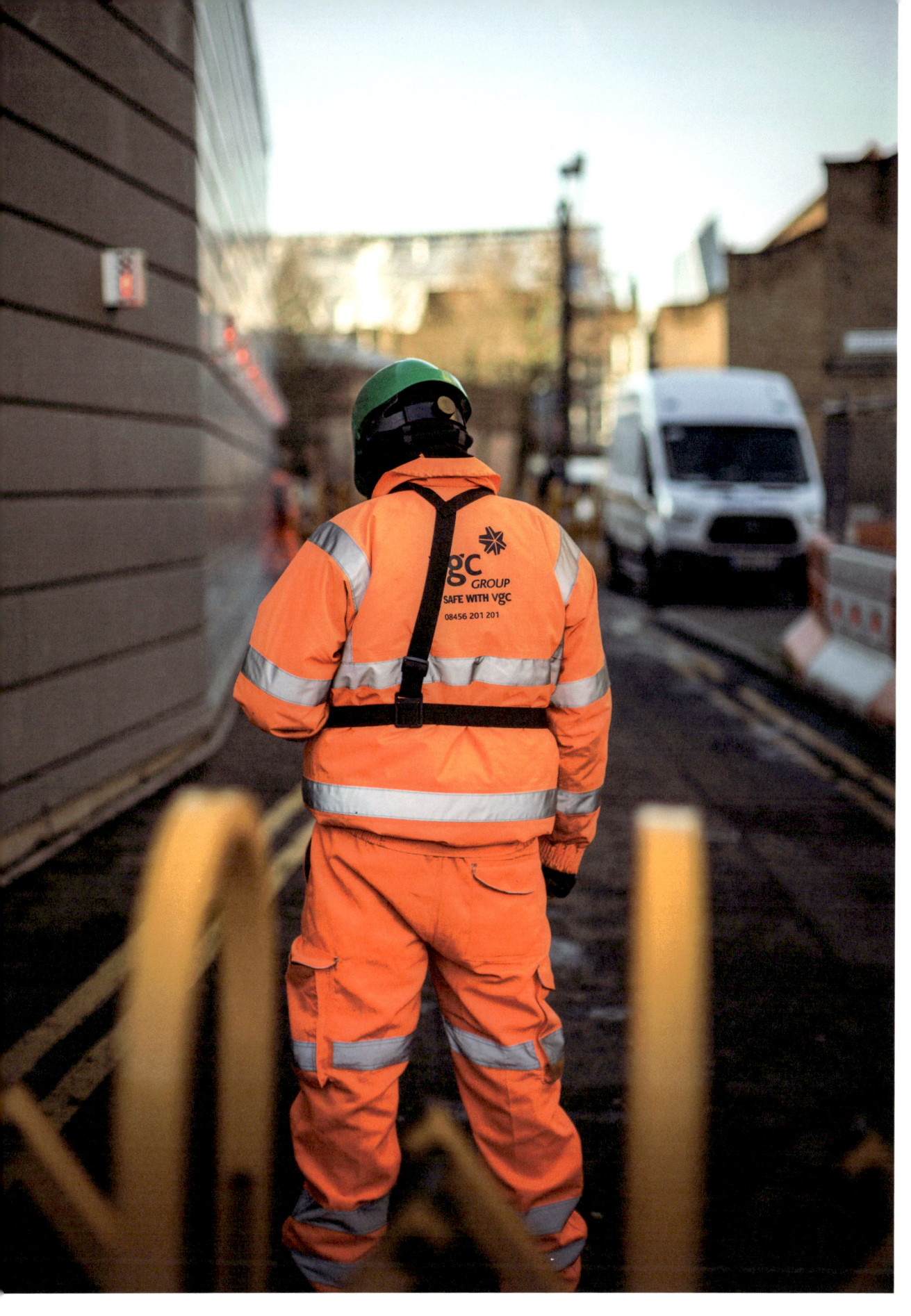

Kristel Parts & Margus Varvas, Mouse Tail Coffee

Tower Hamlets is expected to spike 18 percent over the next decade—the fastest in all of England. Yet the project, which will be over 10 years in the making when the stations and line open this fall, has inadvertently become a visible symptom of the unpopular hyper-development that has come to characterize the city lately.

In what has been coined the "Crossrail Bump," residential real estate prices in the areas surrounding the 10 new stations are set to rise 25 percent by 2021, according to one 2017 study. It is tough to convey just how fast that is—for comparison, that rate outpaces the real estate price increases in suburbs, and London at large. Yet it is worth noting that this development was part of the plan: a large portion of the project's funds derived from special tax assessments and developer contributions. In other words: real estate developers were encouraged to build up around the stations, because it helped pay for the project.

But what that looked like on the ground was another story. Underneath the shadow of rising condos and office buildings are long-standing communities, which will now have to grapple with a shifting landscape—one that includes both an access point that will better connect them to the rest of the city, and also, the influx that comes with it. So I set out to hear from one particular place of business that is enmeshed in each Crossrail community: coffee shops.

I started with Stratford. For a bit of background, Stratford has long been a controversial part of London because it underwent the rite of passage that every Olympic host city bears: the existing neighborhood was largely bulldozed to make way for the Games. Its regeneration brought a maze of high-rises, with more to come. When you leave the Stratford station, it's genuinely difficult to find your way out of the Westfield mall that sits on top of the terminal.

But when I did, I ended up at Sawmill Cafe, a cozy Ukrainian coffee shop just off of the High Street there. A feast of regional delicacies stretched across one table, with smoked fish and cream cheese canapés on full display. I had just missed Lana Zoubata, the cafe's owner, but spoke to her later by phone.

Zoubata said she was busy planning a new specialty coffee and tea shop near the Stratford terminal, which is where the Crossrail station will be located. But she has faced hardship in opening, with high tax rates and rents that are difficult to meet as a small business. "We're fighting," she said. "But of course, it's just easier to open if you're a chain."

I understood what Zoubata meant: at each of the future Crossrail stations I visited, I spotted the usual cadre of London's coffee chains: Pret a Manger, Costa Coffee, Starbucks, and a Tesco Café. The story of local-owned coffee shops struggling to compete against international commercial franchises is, of course, not limited to London. So in Stratford, a neighborhood now defined by its development, the Crossrail seemed like the least of Zoubata's concerns. Rather, for cafe owners like her, it is yet another arbiter of changes that have long been underway here.

"I don't know if Crossrail will change anything here," she admitted. "Because the small businesses are all in the same position."

When I first read about the "Crossrail Bump," news articles cited two communities in particular where the mega-project was speeding up the pace of gentrification: Woolwich and Whitechapel. The area outside of Woolwich Arsenal—a station in southeast London through which the Crossrail will pass—has long been the subject of debates over the city's seemingly unfettered change. A multi-billion-dollar redevelopment of Plumstead Market is the latest source of outrage amongst residents who say the historic community here is being uprooted.

Lucy Paluzsek, artFix Cafe

But at artFix, which is equal parts cafe, community hub, and co-working space, owner George Neris said it is that change that allowed for a place like artFix to exist. "Woolwich is a melting pot in its own right, and people are coming and going all the time," he told me. "We are here to observe the ever-changing mix, and try and bridge the gap between the old and the new."

I asked him what he thinks that melting pot will look like once the Crossrail opens here. "I expect to see a quantum leap," he continued, "both because of Crossrail as well as because of how the the high street experience is changing around the world presently."

Although commuters do not make up much of his business, Neris said, the Crossrail could hold a different effect for him: it will likely usher in a wave of "big coffee and coworking chain brands." (Including those chains I mentioned before, as well as, perhaps, WeWork and Soho House.) That could prove competitive to artFix in the coming years, yet Neris shrugged off the threat. "Those dinosaurs are less agile," he said. "We see this as an interesting challenge to our model."

Contrary to artFix, Mouse Tail Coffee Stories, on Whitechapel High Street, is at its busiest when people are headed to the Whitechapel Tube stop in the morning, said Jamie O'Flynn, a manager there. The tiny coffee shop, which slings cortados and cappuccinos, sits practically out on the sidewalk, nestled in the heart of a bustling Bengali market. O'Flynn said he only expects that foot traffic to increase when the Crossrail opens, as the entrance to the new station will be just down the road.

Whitechapel, to me, is a perfect embodiment of what's happening in London: encouraged by the nearby commercialization of Shoreditch and its famous Brick Lane, the age-old Southeast Asian enclave in Tower Hamlets has been buttressed by encroaching condos and sleek office towers. O'Flynn attested to that change when we spoke: "Whitechapel has seen a huge increase in rent prices in recent years," he told me. "Many of the Bengali community are finding themselves priced out of the area."

O'Flynn said he didn't see that issue going away anytime soon. In fact, he added, it is starting to hit a breaking point. "People are spending more than half of their incomes on rent—not including bills and travel costs—so there have to be some changes soon." But that shouldn't discourage the possibilities that the future holds for London, he argued.

"London has a lot of exciting developments, and now it is probably one of the best cities in the world for coffee these days," he said. "You're never far from a perfect flat white or a great pour over. I'm glad to be part of this."

In the end, Crossrail may hasten change in neighborhoods that look nothing like they did a decade ago—in fact, it already seems like it has. But that should not discount what it says about what London will look like in the coming years; in the end, it is a modern train line to serve new population patterns in a city where people clearly want to be. Perhaps that movement of people will bring more customers to these small cafes, making them more viable against the chains, or encourage more coffee shop owners to consider opening in these neighborhoods, therefore diversifying the landscape. In any case, for coffee, Crossrail seems to be a sign of growth. Full stop.

"Remember, only ten years ago, there was only a handful of specialty coffee shops here," O'Flynn continued. "The industry has really blossomed."

—

Our London

WORDS Laura Steiner
PHOTOGRAPHS Alex Fleming

On the morning of June 27th, 2016, the London Tube was very quiet. Everyone kept their eyes glued to the daily newspaper while the overhead announced we were nearing Holborn. The day before, a majority of voters had voted in favor of the U.K. leaving the European Union. Brexit was now a reality.

The U.K. has historically adopted a policy of multiculturalism around its high number of immigrants. Nowhere is that more obvious than in London—a city filled with people, languages, and traditions from all over the world. In many ways, it is what makes London *London*.

The long-term effects of Brexit are still unclear, but many are concerned about the implications it might have on the U.K.'s immigration policies, and therefore the country's multiculturalism.

Much like a lot of people's experiences with the city, my understanding of London is one of cultural diversity. I moved from Colombia to London in 2014 to do a year-long degree. Fast-forward to 2018 and I am still living here.

Grappling with the possible impact of Brexit on attitudes toward cultural pluralism, I wanted to know more about the people who have migrated to London. Over the course of a week, and over coffee, I learned more about people from different parts of the world, who are part of my own London community and who also call this city home.

Hernando Alvarez

Hernando Alvarez and I meet at the ground floor of BBC, where he has worked as a journalist for the past 18 years. We meet at The Attendant, an unconventionally trendy coffee shop inside of a former public toilet. We sit on what I assume was once upon a time a urinal and today is a high table with grey, velvet chairs.

Alvarez moved from Colombia to London to learn English and what was supposed to be a year-long stay turned into a two-decade love affair with the city he now calls home. That first year, he followed a self-imposed rule where he wasn't allowed to speak anything other than English from Monday to Friday. His favorite pastime was picking a spot on the London Tube and getting off at that station with the aim of "getting lost in the city." Save for his distinctive Colombian twang, he speaks perfect English and he knows London like the palm of his hand.

Does London ever get boring? "You must be mad if this city ever bores you," he says. But, of course, it's never boring for someone who takes pleasure even in the city's most mundane attributes. "My favourite thing is the night bus," he says. "The whole world exists in one of those buses. You hear five, even 10 different languages each night."

Money was tight at first, which meant he had to get creative. "Before playing football, I would do three rounds at the Harrods Food Hall and eat all the sample food and that was lunch!" he laughs. "But I always had enough money for my Guinness after the game."

Daniya "Dani" Asaid and her mother Roqeya Mohammed

I'm on my way to have a Sunday coffee with Dani and her mom. Instead, what I get is a full Sunday lunch with Dani, her mom, her dad, her brothers, one of their wives, and another friend who "is basically a brother" and who has come down from Wales. It's a family affair with a table full of *dolmas*—traditional Kurdish food with vegetables filled with rice and mince. Everyone is speaking over each other in Kurdish and, even though I can't understand a word, this household is lively.

The Asaids moved from Iraq to the United Kingdom 18 years ago and this has been their home since. "Every time I leave London, I want to come back; anywhere else, I feel like a guest," says Roqeya, Dani's mom and the chef behind this feast. Her smile is infectious and I want to tell her that right now is the most at home I have felt in London in a long time.

Stories of growing up in a small town in Iraq are up next on the menu when we're sitting outside on the terrace smoking *shisha* (hookah) and having "the Kurdish version of cigarettes," which are roasted sunflower seeds. Everyone is excitedly speaking over each other and Dani's father who's still inside opens the window only to interject when he hears someone say something erroneous about Kurdish history.

I'm the only one drinking coffee because this household prefers herbal tea and coffee is kept just in case a guest wants one. I leave with the fullest stomach, a head full of facts about Kurdistan, and a plastic container full of Turkish dates, which I am told by Roqeya should never be eaten in even number because "it's bad for your health."

Hernando Alvarez

Daniya Asaid & her mother, Rogeya Mohammed

Lauren Clowes

It's gloomy this Saturday morning, but it's still the very beginning of fall and I ask Lauren Clowes whether she's hot in her double coat combo. "You should see what I wear in winter," she responds. Apparently, she has crafted a "hot water bottle harness" with one bottle in the front and one in the back which makes "everyone here jealous."

By everyone, she means her brother Matthew, who is in charge of the stall behind hers and Marty, who is in charge of the fruit stand next door. We're in Broadway Market where Clowes works every Saturday selling her handmade leather wallets. Her routine is always the same: take the boxes out of the storage, grab a coffee from her favourite coffee place located a few stalls down, and start setting up. By 10:30 a.m., she's high on caffeine and swamped with customers.

Clowes moved down from Manchester 11 years ago. She came down for a party one weekend, ran into a friend who offered her a flat for a good price, and only went back to Manchester—still wearing the same clothes—10 days later to pack up her stuff and move to London. The rest of the story is "boredom," she says. "I had spent too much time in the same place and I was ready for a change."

The change was Hackney and her heart found home in the East London neighborhood. "London is the place where I became an adult and I love it," she says, with a charming northern accent that she definitely hasn't lost over time.

Sabrina Daher

Sabrina Daher is explaining to a customer that filter coffee is going to be oilier than an Americano. She's helping a customer decide on their order. Daher trained as a barista in Sydney and now works in Howl, an East London coffee shop. This French, full-time illustrator and part-time barista is a coffee expert. "It's ironic," she says, "especially considering we don't drink very good coffee in Paris." I am a bit shocked at that statement and she goes on to explain, "In Paris, there's a big thing around coffee. When you say 'Let's go have a coffee,' it means sitting for hours on a terrace with your friends having an espresso. But it's not good coffee," she says. "It's not like London, where people go looking for great coffee."

Daher moved to London six years ago and, while she never expected to fall for the city, it seems she has found her grounding here. "I always thought London was dark, but if you go and dig into it, it's so lively and fun," she says. "It's a tough city, but people are so open-minded here and they're pursuing incredible things."

She turns around to take a new order. It's a South African friend she's drawn a few illustrations for. Daher quickly convinces her to try the filter coffee.

—

London Potters

WORDS John Moore
PHOTOGRAPHS Daniela Velasco

I feel a special connection to London potters like Lucie Rie, one of the most influential potters of the 20th century. She lived and worked in London in her Albion Mews Studio for nearly 60 years beginning in the mid-1930s. Her coffee sets, with their delicate, thin walls and graceful lines, are stunning—exactly the kind of attractive, handmade cups I'd love to pour a brightly flavored coffee in to my warm hands.

Today's potters in London are discovering their own styles, with more city-dwellers than ever before exploring new possibilities and techniques with clay. Open studios, such as Turning Earth, offer space and courses to newcomers pursuing their dreams in clay, while more established potters are fine-tuning their skills in their own workspaces. I treasure visiting their studios, hearing their stories, and finding a new mug, bowl, or plate. Here are four of my favorites.

Stine Dulong

"They just look like they rolled out of the sea," Stine Dulong said excitedly as she showed me two bowls soon after arriving at her studio. The outer surface caught my eye with its slightly rough, gray texture in faint gradations that resembled water soaking into the beach. The tops were asymmetrical and perfectly toasted, and led to a mysterious sea-green, glass-like interior. I immediately had visions of them sitting in front of my fireplace. I have similar coffee mugs and drinking coffee with the pieces in a group would be a beautiful start to the day. Unfortunately, one was sold, and Dulong was keeping the other, so they'll never join my collection at home.

As we were talking, Dulong continued holding and rubbing her hands across the bowls, as though she was still shaping them. It made sense, as Stine prefers hand-building, or coiling, rather than throwing her pottery at the wheel: "My real love lies in coiling, that's when I am happiest. If I could, I would coil every single thing I make." And it shows.

Dulong is the founder of SkandiHus, a ceramics and pottery brand that she creates inside an industrial building in Hackney. It feels luxurious to be in a room in London with such tall ceilings and wide factory windows, and Dulong's studio feels even more so as light fills the space with a magical glow. We simultaneously had the same thought when she said, "I still have to remind myself this is real," in between sips of coffee, as she smiled and looked around the studio.

Dulong did most of her training and practicing at the studio Turning Earth in the evenings, while she was a practicing corporate lawyer by day. Following her passion, she transitioned to become a full-time potter and is now teaching.

Dulong's ceramics, while colorful, have an organic earthy element that I find especially attractive. When I asked how she chooses her colors, she paused before replying, "It is a really funny question as it goes to the core of this constant dilemma I have, because at home I don't have a lot of color. It is almost like there is a need in me to have something more bright and colorful and it comes out in my ceramics. It must be my playful side, as I almost can't help it. A lot of the colors are similar to the seas across the world, particularly my darker blues that are reminiscent of the sea where I grew up on the east coast of Denmark." It was then that I learned Dulong was once a semi-professional sailor, and was twice the Danish champion in her boat class, a very different life from the still moment we were enjoying then. She had to decide between moving to America to become a professional sailor or continuing on with her studies. It looks like she found her calling inland, accompanied by colors from her seafaring days.

Ana (Kana) Kerin

"Can you believe the beauty in this clay?" asked Ana Kerin curiously. Her studio's energetic buzz and her contagious smile made me feel warm and welcomed during the opening of her Nude collection. She makes works of art—think pinch pots and plates with a clear glaze that allows the clay's texture and variations to shine. "They are stunning," I replied as my thumbs unconsciously traced the texture of the clay.

"I am glad you are holding them," she added, "I want my pieces to encourage people to touch them." About the clay, "I'll explain that shortly," she said.

Kerin, the Slovenian-born founder of KANA London, has a playful approach to her work. The coffee mugs I have are a simple, organic shape—small, tapered, and handleless mugs with a dark, coarse finish—made from a chocolate-coffee color glaze on the outside, with a trickle of cream-colored glaze running over the top that resembles milk spilling down the side. It tempts me to start the day on a sweet note with an affogato.

Kerin's love of both food and clay led her to becoming a potter. She was originally a sculptor and shares, "My relationship with food led me to start working with functional ceramics, but in an indirect way. It was through experimental dinners when I thought about the food first rather than the vessel. And that was insightful because afterwards I realized how much I enjoyed working from that angle." She then tells me that, for her chef collaborations, she "imagines the plates from a sculptural perspective, and what would most elevate the food." She was tickled when the restaurant reviews commented on the ceramics together with the food.

I can understand why her ceramics received favorable comments. They have a fun, whimsical feel, which is the same way I imagine her cooking. "I never follow a recipe. I like going to the store and buying random vegetables, spices, and nuts, along with things I have never tried. When I come home, I decide to make rice with raisins and fennel, and then I put in some of this and that, just combining things and mixing them together." My mouth is watering, wishing I could cook like that.

I am holding a blue-gray bowl, my favorite color, when Kerin shares, "I really love simplicity; I only use three glazes and two pigments. These whites are all the same (as she pulls out a small stack of dishes that look very different from each other), but I put them on different colors of clay, or use different layering. I really love playing with combinations like this."

Back to the clay: She has her own proprietary blend of clay that she makes by combining three types together. "That is the only secret recipe I really have," she says.

Left: Pieces by Florian Gadsby. Right: Pieces by Ana Kerin

Pieces by Jono Smart

Pieces by Jono Smart

Florian Gadsby

"The number of mugs I have is over the top—I have around 40 mugs," Florian Gadsby confessed as we were chatting over lunch. I laughed, as I could relate.

Ironically, I do not have one of Florian's mugs, but not for lack of trying. His periodic online shop sells out almost immediately. However, my timing was good during one sale when I could buy an inkwell and dip pen set, which I absolutely cherish. "They are rather romantic to write with. The pen is weighty; it is like using a nice chef's knife," he said. I had just used the pen that morning and was remembering how its balance and texture felt quite calming. He continued, "But they are hard to make. Inherently, they are fragile. They are like a thin ceramic. I had one really bad accident when 20 were on a table and they all rolled on the floor and smashed." He must have seen my look of horror, as he quickly balanced his statement with, "As a potter, you get very good at dealing with things breaking. You become very good at moving on."

When asked how he became interested in ceramics, he said, "I always thought of myself as being a graphic designer." Gadsby's sketches for his pots are as enticing as the pots themselves. He then continued, "My teacher was Caroline Hughes and I remember watching her throw for the first time when she threw a mug. It was really fast—she made it in about 30 seconds! And I thought, 'How do you do that?' And then I had a go and I was rubbish. Then I started throwing more and more, and instead of going out during my lunch break, I would throw pottery. I got hooked. After school, while my friends were playing football, I would throw more pottery. That's how it is with ceramics, it takes a long time to learn."

His glazes have a crackling effect, set against a soft neutral palette of white, blue, gray, and green. Looking at them reminds me of quiet vibrations I feel when walking through freshly fallen snow, its texture and color gently shining in the winter sun. To obtain the color gradations, Gadsby explains that he "adds red iron oxide in the base glaze to become more like a classic celadon color, and with a black iron oxide, it becomes a light blue."

Inside Gadsby's cabinets, what will you find? "None of it is my pottery. Everything I use or own is made by friends, are items I collected, or are gifts I received. And I have a lot of Japanese pots and a large collection of mugs. My mum and dad have always really been into hand-made pots, so I've inherited a lot of their tableware. I get a lot more pleasure eating and drinking from things that are handmade."

In addition to making pottery, Gadsby loves to cook. It is a good thing—he has many nice pots waiting to highlight his food.

Jono Smart

Look at those rich colors! That texture! These are expressions I often hear about Jono Smart's works. When I shared that with him, he happily explained, "My color palette is quite narrow, primarily from white to stone to gray to black, gentle colors that can be part of daily life. I add sand, oxides, and stains directly to the clay to create both the textures and the colors. For most of my works, I leave the exterior unglazed to give them a matte, natural feel, trying to impose as little as possible on the pieces. People rub their hands on them; they want to touch them. I like seeing that and I prefer it to bold statement pieces."

When I wrap my hand around one of his mugs, his signature tab handle fits perfectly against my index finger and makes the cup feel solid in my hand. That handle has become his iconic design. When asked how he plans the shapes of his works, he answers, "I would have never made pots like this had I not done the work before as a garden designer, working for Luciano Giubbilei. He taught me to be a designer. He showed me art. He showed me how to think in that way. So even though the pottery side happened quite quickly over the course of three to five years, the [rest] was 10 years in the making before that."

To get started, Smart also studied and practiced at Turning Earth. He moved away from London in late 2014, but he has deep roots here and he visits often. His studio is now in East Glasgow, at the top of a converted Victorian school, where he has an adjoining studio with his partner Emily Stephen. The recent pairing of their works, Emily's refined wooden bowls (she is a woodturner) sitting so gracefully with Smart's pots and vases, sends shivers up my spine. It speaks to their relationship. "We are constantly talking about and designing new work together and we believe our work is improved through our collaboration. There is a natural harmony between clay and wood, between the tree and the ground it grew from," he shared. They are planning a joint exhibition called "Collected" that will be shown in 2019. I look forward to hearing when it is formally announced, and planning a trip to Scotland.

I was surprised when I first met him because I was expecting someone fairly serious, based solely on his pottery. Instead, he is hilarious, and I especially admire his honesty and bravery. He is a leading advocate for mental health issues and openly shares the obstacles he faces with his own mental health. And while his pottery is so peaceful to hold and admire, it is this authenticity that speaks the loudest in his work.

Pop Up Today, Gone Tomorrow

WORDS Roddy Clarke
FILM PHOTOGRAPHS ON KODAK TRI-X 400 Fabian Schmid

London's busy streets are packed with unique and intriguing retail shops, cafes and stores all vying for the full attention of passersby. With the high-street approach to retail adapting to accommodate a new, wiser shopping generation, the need to stand out is greater than ever before. Every sense has to be attended to, from the scent when one enters to the texture of each surface patrons touch. Over the last several years, pop-ups have kept consumers captivated with unexpected experiences that have been thoughtfully abbreviated to maximize brand identity.

With the U.K. pop-up market now valued at well over £2 billion per year, the temporary, trendy nature of pop-ups suits a new generation of social media-obsessed consumers. Their fleeting presence creates a sense of urgency. The power of social media drives consumers to immerse themselves in trends; strong visuals telegraph a desirable lifestyle.

Businesses can reduce overhead costs with a temporary space, increase hype, and test new niche, consumer markets previously out of reach. Consumers have defined this change. With thousands of pop-up retail spaces in London alone, the capital is leading the way with immersive dining, rotational galleries, and themed design concepts. Pop-ups allow for short-term playfulness that generate buzz and attention online. For example, when the Creme Egg cafe opened in London, the ball pit on its third floor guaranteed interactivity and quick momentum on social media.

London coffee brands such as New North and Pact are mastering this new pop-up generation by collaborating across industries and basing themselves in different locations throughout the year. New North has collaborated with a variety of brands such as Rapha, a cycling company, and Daylesford Organic, an organic farm, and, in 2018, worked as the official coffee partner for London Fashion Week, opening a pop-up store at one of the main entrances to the show. Through this new audience, New North not only increases its own consumer base but also raises its brand profile.

Sevgi Ismailova, Shoreditch High Street Station

Coffee brands and cafes with pop-ups can better immerse into local communities and appeal to wider audiences on a larger scale. Pact, a subscription-based brand, has realized that pop-up stores help carry out vital market research whilst connecting with customers in a personal way, rather than online. Opening in multiple locations helps brands like Pact reach and receive feedback from a much wider audience.

Los Angeles brand Califia Farms, best known for the almond milk many Americans see in barista's hands on cafe bars, is also considering stand alone pop-ups in London. Although stocked in U.K. supermarkets and stores already, Califia Farms milk is better able to connect to U.K. consumers and tease upcoming releases in temporary retail spaces, according to its general manager Brian Lovejoy.

Even though pop-ups enable smaller brands to get cheaper exposure, larger brands that can afford to commit to long-term spaces are also tapping into this new shopping culture by creating temporary spaces within their permanent locations. In the coffee industry, brands are looking at new ways to create interactive experiences outside of normal cafe hours. Benk & Bo, a cafe with an event and working space, collaborates with various partners to offer yoga classes, musical performances, and host events and photoshoots. Offering a membership option, which allows consumers to use the facilities at their leisure, Benk & Bo offers a constant cycle of different events that create buzz and increase foot traffic.

Location is key to a successful pop-up, and Soho and Shoreditch have become particularly desirable host neighborhoods. With high levels of footfall, long shopping hours, and a diverse range of consumers, they are perfect places to experiment with new launches, brands, and products. However, up-and-coming retail areas such as the Oxo Tower on the Southbank have pop-up units attracting brands throughout the year, while Redchurch Street is home to a constant cycle of fresh, design-conscious brands. Areas like this showcase future possibilities for London's retail.

The move towards experiential retail will only become greater. Cafes, restaurants, and brands will all need to innovate to ensure consumers still appreciate a brick and mortar experience. Most brands will need to adapt this approach even within permanent spaces. Permanent pop-up locations such as Boxpark, a permanent collection of pop-up spaces built from storage containers, will become commonplace; visitors will come to expect variety and frequent change. Maybe the next great coffee shop will be virtual, integrating augmented reality to attract customers with unique experiences that will help win a never-ending retail arms race.

—

Market Life

WORDS John Moore
PHOTOGRAPHS Adam Goldberg, Daniela Velasco

The markets in London feature everything you might hope for in a city. I get a real sense of excitement when I plan which markets I will visit—for a snack for the day, breakfast for the coming week, plants to welcome a new season, or a special find for an upcoming birthday. I enjoyed them when I first lived in London 25 years ago, again when I visited after I moved away, and now with my new home on Columbia Road, the location of my favorite market.

COLUMBIA ROAD FLOWER MARKET

A market that has always held a special place in my heart is the Columbia Road Flower Market. The market, open only on Sunday, is beautiful, colorful, and fragrant. With its affordable prices, even more affordable at the end of the day, you will likely find several bunches of flowers in your arms when you leave. But the market is much more than the flowers. Columbia Road and the twisting side streets surrounding it are home to many unique independent shops, some so full that the fun is digging for a special find.

"I love finding hidden places like this," I overheard someone excitedly whisper to her friend inside of Printers & Stationers, a cozy little wine bar tucked behind the market. I smiled, as I had the same thought when I first found it, only to soon realize it was a secret place for many as the lively and friendly crowd, along with their bunches of flowers, spilled out into the street. The energy and buzz made Monday seem so far away.

When I first visited the market over 25 years ago, I was smitten. I can vividly remember the walk from Liverpool Street Station, pondering Charles Dickens's colorful East End characters—like *Oliver Twist*'s Bill Sykes, who I remembered as soon as I hit Bethnal Green Road—and stories with each step. My mom's maiden name was Sikes, and while it was Bill's maliciousness and violence that made him a memorable literary character, his last name also helped. I wondered, "Where did Dickens get the idea for such a character? From around here?" I then picked up the pace, nearly tripping over the broken sidewalk.

*

Growing up, I spent the summers in a quiet, little town north of Dayton, Ohio, nurturing and watching the plants and trees grow, a trait I inherited from my mom. My dad preferred mowing the grass and, while helping him was one of my chores, my passion was taking care of the plants, dreaming they would take over, so I could stop mowing the grass. It wasn't until I reached Columbia Road, lined with its quaint 19th century shops and a road that had been taken over by flowers, plants, and trees that I saw my dream come true. I told myself then: "This is where I must live."

It took several decades for that to happen. After years of watching real estate listings from from faraway Tokyo, only visiting Columbia Road while on short trips to London, I bumped into a friend who mentioned that an apartment right on Columbia Road would soon be up for sale and asked if my partner and I would be interested. "Absolutely," we replied, and anxiously waited for several days while she made arrangements for us to see it. When I first stepped inside and saw the view from the windows over the market, my heart started racing. The building was an old furniture factory and the top floor was wide open with windows on both ends facing north and south, balanced with a fireplace in the middle of the floor. The kitchen was huge; it started from the fireplace and ran along both walls, framing the view onto Columbia Road. I had visions of making and drinking coffee there in the mornings, and on Sundays, sipping my first cup while watching the traders set up their stalls. I have realized most of that vision, although I now tend to stay curled up in bed at 4 a.m. while the traders are setting up. Once I am up and in the kitchen, I still love listening to the traders

shouting their wares and comments—many more colorful than the flowers. My Sunday routine now starts after my first cup of coffee, when I go downstairs to browse the flower stalls. Just outside the door, there is a large stall, owned by Carl, that primarily sells herbs, which perfume the air with the most intoxicating aroma of mint, rosemary, and lavender. To the right, there is Stuart, who stocks his stall with orchids of all shapes and sizes. A stall further up the road specializes in bulbs. Surrounding these are many others offering a variety of cut flowers, plants, and trees. Around 6:30 a.m., it is serene and quiet, with the flowers arranged and ready to go to their new homes.

I am often asked if I have any favorite stalls, but the market really is a case of the whole being greater than the sum of its parts. I do, however, spend a lot of time at a stall owned by Lyndon Osborn, a New Zealander specializing in unusual outdoor plants. He is easy to talk with and offers genuine, easy-to-follow advice for plant maintenance. The tree ferns he imports are stunning and would make excellent additions to an outdoor terrace, if I had one. Until then, I buy his scented geraniums, as they have the deepest, richest fragrance. I keep several pots inside and, when I pass them, I pause and rub my fingers on the leaves; the aroma is so soothing. I learned early on that Osborn has a strong following with many arriving at 7 a.m. for the best selection. If he has stepped away to get breakfast, his customers wait at his stall until he returns. It is one of the few times when I have seen people patiently waiting in London.

After browsing the market, it is time to get some breakfast: sausage and egg rolls sold out of an unnamed stand in a little yard on Ezra Street just behind Columbia Road. It's only open during the market. The rolls are prepared on a humble grill tucked away in the yard's back left corner, where departing customers have huge smiles on their faces accompanying the huge rolls in their hands. I think of my dad as I wait in line. He had routine weekend breakfast habits that did not make sense to me then—but now I understand.

On the way back to Columbia Road, I turn right into The Courtyard, which feels like a secret hideaway, with little shops lining its four walls. Straight ahead in the right corner is Lily Vanilli Bakery, my favorite bakery, selling pastries even more colorful and aromatic than the flowers outside. During the week, I can hear deliveries made to her shop; I look out the window and see the pitched roof of the Columbia Primary School next door, and then look down and see a Dickensian deliveryman pushing a trolley of flour to the bakery. Also in The Courtyard is the back entrance to Milagros, a shop with handmade products from Mexico. In the colder months, on Sundays, the owners' (Tom and Juliette) daughter sells Mexican hot chocolate just outside the door. A chocolate brownie from Lily Vanilli's, paired with a cup of hot chocolate from Milagros helps ward off the cold, damp London air.

I then head back out on Columbia Road where just behind the flower stalls are rows of independent shops. When I look for temptation, I go to:

Pavilion Bakery: This is potentially the most inviting and delicious coffee shop on Columbia Road. Pavilion is first and foremost a bakery. While its cardamom buns are delicious, it is the dense, tangy white sourdough bread that gets me. One slice toasted and topped with melted butter perfectly complements a cup of coffee. I opt for Pavilion's flat whites, the milk gives way to the rich flavor of house-roasted beans.

Mason & Painter: I love vintage goods and Michelle Mason's little gem of a shop is a dream. I always find something, be it an old breadboard, a zinc pitcher with perfect patina, or an old book filled with useful advice. If I had more space, Masons's wooden tables and garden chairs along with the pillows she makes from vintage fabrics would be coming home with me. Her shop has two entrances with the backdoor opening into The Courtyard (near Lily Vanilli). Make sure you look back there, where she also keeps additional stock; the best items tend to hide in the back.

Glitterati: I am weak around vintage Champagne coupes, so I was both thrilled and worried when I first saw this shop, just a few doors down from me, stocking an excellent selection of antique glassware and cufflinks (another weakness). While out of my league, there is a well-edited selection of vintage couture jewelry, hats, and bags. The shop can get crowded, and it used to be my natural instinct to return later when it was less so. However, I am still kicking myself for doing that when a perfect set of six Champagne coupes with hollow stems (my favorite style) was shining brightly in the window. It was my first and last time to see such a set.

Columbia Pottery: I adore Victorian clay pots with notable patina. I find they always look settled on a windowsill holding basil, mint, or scented geraniums. This shop, filled with many odds and ends, is deceiving at first. To find the Victorian pots, go to the back of the shop in the little enclosed garden. Chris, the owner, prices them reasonably, which means they sell quickly, especially the larger ones. Stylists keep their eyes open for these, as they make stunning table arrangements for any occasion. If you see one you like, grab it.

Vintage Heaven: Here is another vintage shop worth visiting, with stacks of plates and other tableware displayed throughout the store. Although the plates are beautiful, I tread carefully to the back right corner, just at the entrance to the Cake Hole Café, to a small but promising collection of kitchen goods. It is in this little corner where I have found some of the best vintage bread pans, muffin tins, and silverware in London—and all for reasonable prices. To note, Margaret Willis, the owner, is a great conversationalist with many good stories to share.

Shopped out, I head back to Ezra Street to where it splits in three directions and forms my favorite little spot in London. At this small intersection, you'll find a little hole in the wall (literally) where the Oyster Boy, Conor Pearson, shucks oysters to pair with his bloody marys or, as Pearson taught me, to enjoy with a Guinness stout. The sweetness in the oyster mellowed the stout's bitter finish, leaving a creamy texture that had me craving another. It is a very appropriate East London snack.

To wrap up the day, I cross Ezra Street and walk into the coziest and most inviting wine bar, Printers & Stationers. I have known Augustin, the owner, and his shop since 2008 and witnessed its many changes. He started selling antiques, which I miss as he has exquisite taste. Over the years, he transitioned it to a wine bar and supper club, which I always took the time to visit when I was in London. He took a few years off and is restarting with a delicious choice of wines and teas to drink there or take home. He is originally from the Champagne region, and it shows, as there is always a delicious champagne being served by the glass. Enjoying a glass with a plate of cheese while listening to the buskers performing outside has been a main feature of my Sunday creature-of-habit routine, long before I lived here. This is my favorite little spot in London.

As for the walk back to Liverpool Street Station, while no longer on my itinerary, I still walk halfway there, down to Redchurch Street and into the home of Allpress Espresso. Its beans are top notch and all of its coffee brew choices are good. My preferred choice is Allpress' pour over. Hearing the whir of coffee grinder, watching the spiral pour of the water, and finally tasting a very delicate yet complex cup of coffee, is a perfect accent to the day. Now it is time to go home and tend to the plants and flowers patiently waiting for me.

Pavilion Bakery

Columbia Road Flower Market: Open on Sunday from 7 a.m. to 3 p.m. The main market is located between Ravenscroft Street and Barnet Grove, with more to explore on the side streets. In addition, on the four Wednesday evenings preceding Christmas Day, Christmas Wednesday Shopping Evenings are held when the stores are open until 9 p.m.

Pavilion Coffee and Bakery: Located at 130 Columbia Road. Open daily from 7 a.m.

Allpress Espresso: Located at 58 Redchurch Street in Shoreditch. It is open Monday–Friday, 7:30 a.m. to 5 p.m., and Saturday–Sunday, 9 a.m. to 5 p.m.

MARYLEBONE FARMERS' MARKET

This market was a surprise when I found it. It is only open on Sunday, from 10 a.m. to 2 p.m., and I happened to stumble across it when I was visiting London and went to Marylebone on a Sunday afternoon for an unrelated reason. Quality over quantity is the rule here, as the market is limited to 40 stalls stocked with beautiful fresh vegetables, herbs, eggs, cheese, bread, fish, meat, and baked goods. I initially bought some baked goods. Over time, I tried other goods I could keep in the hotel room and eat throughout the week.

Now that I have an apartment, when I am in the mood for a traditional Sunday supper at home but not in the mood to cook, I take the bus over to this market and walk straight to the stall by Madame Gautier, whose freshly made Pot Roasted Chickens à l'Ancienne make my mouth water. The chickens are stuffed with everything wonderful—sage, onion, garlic—and served in a rich wine sauce. I take this home, along with some potatoes and vegetables, and arrange them on rustic dishes set on top of old serving boards for an impromptu feast. The chicken is sold warm so even when I was visiting London, I would take it to my hotel room for a hearty dinner. In the cooler months, I also get the Confit de Boeuf to warm up later during the week.

For dessert, I love the cakes from Honeypie Bakery. Valerie's selections change with the season and it is exciting to see what she bakes for the market. Her Lemon & Lavender and Plum & Raspberry cakes are two of my favorites. I also get at least one slice of the Coffee & Walnut cake when she has it. While I like eating these cakes for dessert, I like them even better with coffee in the morning. It is a great start to the day.

After the market, as I am walking down to Oxford Street to get the bus, I stop at Workshop Coffee on Barrett Street, just off St. Christopher Place. Workshop Coffee has several locations and this little outpost is a nice surprise. Relaxing with one of their rich espressos is a pleasant finish to an afternoon in Central London.

Marylebone Farmers' Market: Open on Sunday from 10 a.m. to 2 p.m. The market is located on Aybrook, St. Vincent, and Moxon Streets, just off Marylebone High Street.

Workshop Coffee: Located at 1 Barrett Street in Marylebone, just north of Oxford Street. It is open Monday–Friday, 7 a.m. to 7 p.m., and Saturday–Sunday, 9 a.m. to 6 p.m.

BROADWAY MARKET

I had heard about Broadway Market before I first visited. While relatively close to Columbia Road (about a 10 minute walk), this market is held on Saturdays. The choices of prepared food as well as raw food to cook at home is staggering. It's hard to know where to begin. Over the last few years, I have found myself gravitating towards the same places, although I force myself to try something new each time.

One of the first places I tried was The Frenchie, selling duck confit burgers. The name and the signboard is what first caught my attention. When I saw and smelled the burgers, which came with a choice of blue, smoked cheddar, or goat cheese, I was sold. To top it off, I could get a side of duck fat chips. I chose the blue cheese and an order of chips. I was still full when it came time for dinner. My eyes were much bigger than my stomach; since then, I've limited myself to half a sandwich and stay away from the fries. Although, when someone else orders fries, I am more than happy to have one or two.

It is hard for me to resist cheese, especially French cheese, and the large display by La Bouche is impossible to miss. I have tried all of their cheeses and keep going back for more. In the winter months, I especially like the raclette melted on a slice of toasted sourdough from Pavilion, a nearby bread stand. In the warmer months, I could have a meal eating only La Bouche's goat cheese.

The stall called Downland Produce is also a regular stop. It first caught my attention as they sell my favorite yogurt, Hurdlebrook Guernsey Wholemilk Yoghurt, and the "Forest Fruits" flavor at that. I later tried their eggs, then chicken, and recently the pork. All are fresh and delicious.

When I want something healthier, Fin & Flounder has the best seafood shop. If you tell the fishmonger that you want to have sashimi, they will bring up special cuts of salmon and tuna, depending on your preference. When I first ate the salmon I thought, "This tastes better than the sashimi in Japan," and I was living in Japan. Then one day, it suddenly dawned on me that the sashimi in Japan has been on a boat traveling from Norway or Scotland. Of course this sashimi is better in London; it is often fresher. Fin & Flounder also has a stall in the market and, while I am not the biggest fan of waiting in lines, I do wait in line for the Lobster Brioche Roll, especially in the summer as something about lobster rolls just feels like my childhood summers.

As for a new discovery, I recently tried the mini cinnamon rolls from Centanni. The only thing better than the cinnamon rolls is having them with Climpson & Sons coffee, either from its flagship store or its coffee cart in the market. I prefer any of their single origins and, in addition to buying a cup to splurge with the rolls, I usually get a bag of beans too, to enjoy during the week. Now, if I could only find some cinnamon rolls to enjoy during the week too.

Broadway Market: Open on Saturday from 9 a.m. to 5 p.m. The market is located on Broadway Market between Regent's Canal and London Fields.

Climpson & Sons Coffee: Located at 67 Broadway Market. It is open Monday–Friday, 7:30 a.m. to 5 p.m.; Saturday, 8:30 a.m. to 5 p.m.; Sunday, 9 a.m. to 5 p.m.
—

Lili Vanilli Bakery

Master of Reinvention

WORDS Andy Greeves
PHOTOGRAPHS Daniela Velasco

Despite its proximity to the City of London, Shoreditch was—until recent decades—somewhere that few Londoners, let alone visitors to the capital, ever ventured. Widespread deindustrialisation left the majority of Victorian factory spaces in this particular part of the East End empty by the end of the 1970s, and the area became an abandoned relic.

The seeds for the vibrant, colourful, and edgy Shoreditch of today were first sewn in the 1980s, as artists, fashion designers, and fellow creatives started to move to the area, lured by the availability of large studio spaces at reasonable rates. Notable examples include Steve Edge—affectionately known as "Lord Shoreditch"—who established his advertising agency Edge Design (with clients like the upmarket department store Fortnum & Mason) in the area in 1982, and Richard Boote, who toured with The Who, Pink Floyd, and David Bowie, and opened the Strongroom recording studios off Curtain Road in 1984, producing albums by The Chemical Brothers and even the first Spice Girls album. Both businesses are still there today.

Another seminal moment came following the closure of the Black Eagle Brewery—also known as Truman Brewery—on Brick Lane in 1989. Bars, restaurants, shops, and markets soon popped up in the vacant space. Today, the Old Truman Brewery has become East London's creative hub, with more than 700 businesses housed there, including fashion designers, advertising agencies, and architecture firms as well as recording and photographic studios.

Defining Shoreditch's exact boundaries with neighbouring parts of the capital, such as Bethnal Green, Haggerston, and Spitalfields, is a tricky task. Roughly speaking, its most westerly point is Old Street roundabout, while Brick Lane runs along its easterly "boundary." You'll be heading out of the neighborhood somewhere along Kingsland Road to the north and Commercial Road to the south.

More than any other part of the capital, Shoreditch is a living, breathing canvas for street art. The graffiti artist Banksy has executed numerous works in the area over the years, including "A Girl and Balloon" and "Guard Dog," while his "Snorting Copper" was recently returned to public view at its original 2006 location at 115 Curtain Road. Alas, many of his (and other street artists') works have been painted over by local councils of Hackney and Tower Hamlets over the years, or removed by developers. The street art scene in Shoreditch is very much "here today, gone tomorrow."

The aforementioned Strongroom recording studios have seen artists such as Nick Cave, Radiohead, The Prodigy, and Rufus Wainwright record iconic albums, while another local studio above Shoreditch Grind espresso bar has been graced by the likes of Sam Smith, Tinie Tempah, and Hurts. Aside from music, art, fashion, and design, Shoreditch has also, in the last decade, become London's epicentre for high-tech companies. Indeed, the area has acquired the nickname "Silicon Valley," while Old Street roundabout—where many of these technology firms are based—has been dubbed "Silicon Roundabout."

With Shoreditch such a bright beacon of creativity, individuals and businesses alike feel a strong draw to the area. And the large numbers of creatives still in the area suggests it is clinging on to the vibrant, artsy scene pioneered 30 or so years ago, despite the damage tourists and big corporations have done to Shoreditch's cultural and creative credentials.

Shoreditch is a pioneer and a leader of so many of London's creative scenes and the coffee culture here is as prevalent—if not more so—than any other part of the capital. While the "posh" parts of West London—Chelsea, Kensington, and so on—are still home to strong afternoon tea-drinking traditions, the East End runs on coffee. Fix 126 on Curtain Road is a favourite haunt of the students of the nearby fashion college, while Coffee Junction at 42 Provost Street appeared in the BBC smash

COFFEE		FOOD	
ESPRESSO	2.30	MIXED PLATE	
MACCHIATO	2.30	EGG, AVOCADO, PROVOLONE,	
PICCOLO, CORTADO	2.50	TOMATO	9.00
LONG BLACK	2.50	-JAMON	ADD 2.50
FLAT WHITE	2.90	-SALMON	ADD 3.00
LATTE	2.90	SALMON TOAST & GOATS CURD	5.00
CAPPUCCINO	2.90	EGGS & SOLDIERS	5.50
MOCHA	3.00		
HOT CHOCOLATE	3.00	TOAST & AVOCADO	4.50
LARGE, DECAF	.50	TOAST	
OAT MILK	.30	-MARMALADE	
BATCH BREW	2.50	-JAM	
TEA	2.60	-LEMON CURD	3.00
YORKSHIRE, EARL GREY			
FRESH MINT		BUCKWHEAT GRANOLA WITH	
ORANGE JUICE	3.50	POACHED FRUIT & YOGHURT	5.50
APPLE/BEETROOT JUICE	2.50	PANINO	2.50
LEMONADE	3.50		
ICED COFFEE	3.00		
COLD BREW	3.00		
MAZAGRAN	3.00		

Bodyguard earlier this year. Café 1001 is part of Brick Lane's vibrant clubbing scene by night and by day, a laid-back hangout for comfort foods and caffeine.

Origin—one of the U.K.'s largest speciality coffee roasters—was established in Cornwall in 2004. Such was the appeal of Shoreditch that it decided to open its flagship location on Charlotte Road in 2015, showcasing its ever-changing range of single origin coffees whilst hosting barista training and technical support for London customers. "At Origin, art and creativity run deep," explains Alice Tieu, who is the general manager at Charlotte Road. "The vibrancy of Shoreditch and strong creative influences from local businesses and area footfall originally drew Origin, inspiring the Charlotte Road set up."

"I'd describe the area as a mixed bag of all sorts of creative influences. There are a lot of young freelance professionals in the area that specialise in the creative industry. Alongside this, there are often many innovative projects and events taking place within the local area— an example of this would be the Digital Shoreditch Program. The programme is comprised of an industry-led community celebrating and promoting the creative, technical, and entrepreneurial talent of London."

Workshop Coffee also found the lure of Shoreditch unavoidable, opening a coffee bar at the White Collar Factory on Old Street roundabout. "Shoreditch continues to be an exciting, continually evolving area of London," says Workshop's head of marketing and retail Richard Frazier. "Old Street literally sits at the intersection of the well-established city firms, start-ups of various sizes and at varying stages of growth, an increasing number of coworking spaces and, of course, the renowned creative reputation of Shoreditch. It was this, along with the White Collar Factory development itself, that drew us to the area. The ambitious building, which was brought to life by London-based developers Derwent takes inspiration from the work of self-taught French designer Jean Prouvé and makes for a unique, beautifully executed space. There's is an open-air, 200-meter running track that winds around the 17th floor. It's an unnecessary but utterly fantastic detail that tells you everything you need to know about the people that designed the building and the people that were likely to be drawn to it."

Shoreditch has grown at an exponential rate over the last few decades especially, and while the area has its many supporters, there are also detractors. A satirical fanzine called *Shoreditch Twat*—published between 1999 and 2004—captured, according to local resident Lida Hujic, "the moment when the organic community began to be infiltrated by types whose intentions were dubious. The *Shoreditch Twat* distinguished between the genuine creatives who were drawn to the area in search of similarly minded people and the fakes—opportunists who wanted to cash in on this creative hub, or *faux artistes* pretending to be scruffy and yet having loads of money from their parents."

The area has been lambasted by those who see it as a leading example of the gentrification of London. "Shoreditch is a formula, a brand," wrote journalist Alex Proud in *The Telegraph* back in 2014. He called for the end of the "Shoreditchification" of the capital. "Shoreditch is just a metonym for all those unlucky pieces of real estate that have had the hipster formula applied to them. It's as much a part of mainstream consumer culture as iPhones and Sky TV, and as global as Starbucks."

For all the criticism levelled at Shoreditch—and looking beyond the many stereotypes about it—there remains a genuine feeling of community in this part of London. Another of the nicknames Shoreditch has garnered over the years is "The Village," which reflects the feeling of closeness shared by those who live, work, and even visit the area.

The strength of community here is reflected in a social enterprise called Spitalfields Crypt Trust (SCT). Established in 1965, the Trust has been supporting people recovering from addiction by helping them to get clean and sober, build self-respect, and hope for a brighter future. The most visible example of its work is in its coffee-bookshop at 18 Calvert Avenue. Manager Anna Krukowska explains: "I've worked at Paper & Cup for the last four years, and what has made me stay is the opportunity to help vulnerable adults get their lives back on track. Our coffee shop has been set up by SCT charity to train people in recovery from alcohol and other addictions, to increase their employability." SCT also serves as a drop-in centre for the homeless—a vital service for the community at a time in which there has been a 169% rise in homelessness in the United Kingdom since 2010. The charity's connection with the local area has always been unwavering—even during periods in which people were moving away from Shoreditch. Krukowska shares SCT's admiration for this particular part of the East End and the customers she serves: "SCT is based in Shoreditch, and have been working there for over 50 years, so naturally we want to be in the area we affected the most."

"The beauty of Shoreditch is in all the different cultures and businesses mixing close by. We have a lot of regular customers in our shop, but mostly they are young professionals from nearby businesses. Some people have been coming since we opened, and it is always nice to see familiar faces."

AIDA—an independent concept store on Shoreditch High Street that combines Scandinavian-inspired clothing and homewares—offers a series of Wonder Lattes in its onsite cafe. Its collection of brightly coloured concoctions includes the visually arresting Rose Latte—which is flavoured with rose syrup and given its distinctive pink hue with organic beetroot juice.

Numerous overseas coffee companies have made Shoreditch their U.K. home, including New Zealand roaster Allpress Espresso, which started up its London operation on Redchurch Street in Shoreditch back in 2010. Compatriot Ozone has a roastery, coffee bar, and eatery at 11 Leonard Street. And of course, the U.K.'s biggest annual celebration of coffee is held in Shoreditch. The London Coffee Festival was in its ninth year when it returned to the Old Truman Brewery in March of 2019.

—

An Unexpected Luxury: Q&A with Richard Frazier and Jason Catifeoglou

INTERVIEW & PHOTOGRAPHS
Adam Goldberg, Daniela Velasco

Don't look for a stuffy lobby with a formal check-in desk when you arrive at The Pilgrm Hotel in Paddington. You'll be met instead by an outpost of Workshop Coffee. It is a surrogate welcome area, a place to check in, a meeting location, and an external living room—a lobby by any standards, but with much better coffee.

For anyone who has ever suffered through insipid in-room instant brews or bottomless pitchers of cardboard drip at a hotel restaurant, this is a blessing. As a new kind of hotel catering to a new kind of traveler, The Pilgrm never imagined anything less than stellar coffee served throughout the hotel: The partnership with Workshop Coffee was part of the plan from the beginning.

Workshop, which has been instrumental in building the London coffee scene since it opened its first location in 2011, has been part of the city's widespread embrace of coffee as an integral part of hospitality. While it might be unheard of for a five-star hotel in other major cities to think about its coffee program with as much focus as it does its food, even Claridge's in London partners with Workshop for a custom coffee program, proudly listing the vendor on its menus. The Mandarin Oriental, The Ned, The Ace Hotel, and others have also followed suit, at last taking their coffee programs as seriously as they do everything else.

As Richard Frazier, head of retail and marketing at Workshop Coffee, and Jason Catifeoglou, co-owner of The Pilgrm Hotel, describe in a recent interview, modern hotels have to live up to the tastes of young travelers, who expect great coffee in a fun, creative atmosphere the same way they expect well-appointed fitness facilities and USB ports next to the bed. Below, Frazier and Catifeoglou talk more about how the partnership came to be and how, in 2019, hotels are learning that showcasing quality ingredients extends to coffee too.

How did you guys get into the hotel business?
Jason: I did a degree in furniture design here in London and I thought it was meant to be the thing that I do. But then I met my current business partner at the time, who had a hotel in London. I went to have a look at it, because it was all designed by [English designer and restaurateur Terence] Conran. I went in wide-eyed, looking at the spaces, design, and furniture and whatnot, and I fell in love with it. That was it really. A good 20-odd years later, here we are.

When you were designing the hotel, were there any key elements that you had in mind beforehand?
Jason: Yes. I mean, the notion of turning the hotel experience upside-down and removing all of the—what we described as unnecessary items—such as the minibars, the coffee facilities, etc. But, when we say removing them, we mean taking them out of the room and putting them somewhere else and really emphasising the quality. In order to do that, we had to sacrifice certain aspects. What was absolutely non-negotiable was the fact that we were going to recycle, find reclaimed timbers, radiators, and marbles and restore and repurpose them, which is not easy. That was the tricky bit. As an idea, it's lovely, but actually delivering is a whole new story.

How do you think hotel hospitality has changed over the last 20 years? In talking to people and travelling around the world, we've learned that people want to have that slightly more seamless experience without the noise. There's enough going on out there to be a little bit more humble when you arrive at a hotel. Why do people want an Airbnb? It's another experience that's very different than at a hotel, and that was our sort of aim. How do you bring the two together? The Airbnb experience with the hotel services and facilities and all of that.

Has the idea of luxury changed? As a traveller, if I see speciality coffee and reclaimed materials, that's a new kind of luxury. Whereas, maybe 20 years ago, it might have been gold leaf and chandeliers.
Jason: Massively. One of our mottoes is luxury from unexpected places. So how do you present luxury in a new and modern way for the modern traveller? And that's not about the gold leaf—you appreciate luxury through materials, through experience, through human interaction. How do you present that today in a new way but also through ingredients and sourcing and doing things really, really well without them being too loud?

When did the integration of a specialty coffee experience come into the development of the hotel?
Jason: We were discussing Workshop from the very beginning: How do we integrate the best possible coffee experience downstairs? The best possible cocktail food or rooms? Everything was all about doing less but doing it really, really well. And we opened by doing the downstairs coffee shop ourselves; that was just to get us over the line with issues with building work. It was very obvious that at some point we would have to get these guys on board and bring it to the next level. It was only a matter of time. But it was very much from the beginning that we knew we had to do something special.

And how did you guys meet?
Richard: This is kind of the secondary stage to our relationship.

Jason: So I used to own a business across the road called The Zetter on the corner of St. Johns Square where the original Workshop was. That was my hangout and meeting place, and I always loved it. A lot of the creation of this happened in that spot on the coffee bar. Tasting the coffee was all about the site; it speaks of what you see here today. It's the narrow entrance, small and discreet street front, but then it opens up, so we thought: What would happen if there were bedrooms upstairs instead of a restaurant? A lot of it was inspired from that one site. I met James, founder and CEO of Workshop, back then. So we've always been talking about how we've got to do something together and this was the perfect timing.

Do you think the guests notice that there's a specialty coffee program?
Jason: For our audience, it's crucial. People appreciate it. They understand quality these days. It's not like you need to oversell it. You see it in people's faces instantly as soon as they try it. We've got a whole new audience that's just dropping in to get a coffee or staying here because of the fact that we've got Workshop here. It's amazing how important it is for everybody.

Why do you think it's so rare to find specialty coffee in a hotel experience?
Jason: Perhaps it comes as a secondary thing though in most cases. Now, I don't know how you're seeing it from talking to hoteliers when you go in as a wholesale supplier. But, with anybody that I am interacting with in the hotel world, it's always, "Oh, we have to do coffee, so let's find a wholesale supplier," rather than how we've done it, which is a complete integration. It's a joint venture almost. It's a partnership and we're making it work for both of us. You see that a lot in the United States where they're doing so much to bring coffee experiences to that level.

Richard: I think it sounds like a sort of backhanded comment or an off-hand comment to say that it's an afterthought, but it is in the way that your bread and butter isn't serving coffee. It's just one small component of what you do and it's the same with any hotel or business that isn't a cafe, coffee shop, or coffee bar. But that's changing, because I think people are becoming more aware of it from the business side of things in terms of what can be offered and how it can enhance the overall experience. The other side at play is this whole rising tide raises all ships mentality, where people's expectations of what constitutes not a great or the best coffee that you can have but just a good cup of coffee. It's just so much more accessible. And it's great that places like Claridge's are being forward-thinking enough to recognise that now as opposed to clambering to figure it out and respond when it's sort of too late. You're moving with that trend and those expectations rather than trying to catch up to them. It comes down to people's expectations and where the benchmark sits within the market now for coffee.

There are so many factors at play, and it's not just specific to hotels either. Restaurants are maybe a half-step ahead, but I think it's true of restaurants as well. In most places, you end up getting your after-dinner espresso and it very much feels like an afterthought when you know that so much attention, care, and detail has been paid to every component and every element of that dish.

I think people are a little bit afraid of A) getting it right in the first instance, and B) maybe the cost and time involved from a training and staffing perspective. It's like, "Oh, God. Are we even going to be able to do it right? Is it better that we just deal with the devil that we know and understand?"

If a hotel wants to put together a specialty coffee program, in the simplest form, what might you recommend that they do?
Richard: First, you need to understand what it is that they actually want from the program. Do they want consistency? Do they want to be showcasing what unusual coffees that there are available? There might be different objectives depending on the size and the nature of their hotel. But I think that the biggest thing I'd ask that they consider is training. Find someone—not just who can help you get the quality product into the building but can actually help you, your staff, the people who are going to be serving it—to understand that product, know how to use it, and troubleshoot. Those are the invaluable elements. Identify people within businesses and those hotels or spaces—whatever it might be—who can actually be the go-to, the point guard from a coffee point of view.

Richard Frazier & Jason Catifeoglou, Workshop Coffee at The Pilgrm

I would love to brew delicious, really consistent, filtered coffee with fairly minimum investment from a training and an equipment point of view, 100 percent. But again, you've got that other factor at play which is the market, which is the customer, which are guest expectations, and when you're a hotel, you are looking to meet and exceed people's expectations. They want to enjoy themselves and indulge, and the customer—this is only from a U.K. point of view—most of the time, is looking for an espresso-based drink. When they think coffee, they think cappuccino, espresso, or any variance on those elements. In other places, you've got people who are very much expecting to be a *carte blanche*: pick their espresso or type of coffee, pick their milk, pick all manner of things, and that is part of their experience and expectations when they show up at the door and get their room key.

What are the most popular drinks that customers order?
Richard: Here, the espresso-based drinks, so flat whites and cappuccinos, are probably our biggest sellers, but the filter's really great. We're massive proponents of filter. At The Pilgrm specifically, we only do batch brew. It's perfect for the environment and the nature of the space, and the one extra element that you have is to be able to offer samples. You can't do that with a V6 or an AeroPress in the same way. It's a perfect conversation point. It's what people want. It's a great vessel for coffee.

With filter coffee, it's a bit easier to maintain consistency. How do you ensure that the espresso drinks remain consistent?
Richard: When we're talking about our coffee bars, obviously our baristas and our supervisors and managers are all trained and have been with us since they got into coffee. Our barista roadmap sees people joining as barbacks. It takes about six months before they actually get behind a machine and pop a shot. And that's only in our training space, so we're not looking for people that are experienced in coffee, necessarily. We're looking for the right kind of people with the right kind of attitude to give them the skills and teach them to make coffee. That's kind of how we ensure consistency. And we have our quality control and quality monitoring program in place that they carry out across the bars on a daily basis, whether it's with the water checks, whether it's using refractometers. We keep the geekery out of sight.

For a new hotel that wants to put together a coffee program, is there really a big cost difference between specialty coffee and commodity coffee?
Richard: Of course, there is, because the quality of the raw ingredients is higher and there are additional costs involved when it comes to the quality control processes and the stages that are actually happening in the roastery when we're roasting the coffee. But ultimately, the difference isn't enormous. It is isn't a chasm between the two. You're talking a few extra pence a cup rather than pounds upon pounds, which is mental really when you think about it. I think where the more commodity based stuff tends to win is the free on-loan equipment stuff. That's the real draw.

Is there anything that you're particularly proud of with the coffee program here?
Richard: The fluidity I was talking about before between the space and the hotel and the coffee bar. They're not siloed. They're not separate entities. They work together, and I think that works really, really well whether you're staying at the hotel as a guest or whether you're just visiting from down the road.

To me, the answer to that is the partnership. That's what's beautiful about it, and we've started up here. We don't have to think of this hard line between Workshop and The Pilgrm. The teams are now one. Workshop has become a byword for quality, which is something we're really, really proud of. I'm absolutely thrilled for it.

How did you connect with Claridge's?
Richard: About 14 months ago, they were tending to their coffee program and looking to elevate it. They came to us talking about guest expectations, looking to exceed them and also anticipate them so do something a little bit different with their coffee program. It was a fairly intense sort of process. It was various conversations and various meetings, but after a few months we got through and then went in. In the middle of the night, we installed the espresso machines and grinders, and we were up and running for breakfast the following morning. And it was just that black and white of a switchover, which was pretty cool.

If you had to summarise the specialty coffee scene in London, how would you describe it?
Richard: "Booming" is probably the one word that encapsulates it in terms of the number of roasters, the number of cafes and coffee bars, and coffee-focused spaces that you have. It's a really interesting time for specialty coffee in London. I think we're at a—I don't know if I'd call it a tipping point or not, but the fact that we're sitting here and we're having a conversation about Workshop Coffee and specialty coffee in general popping up in places where even two years ago you just wouldn't have seen it in hotels and office spaces. The way that the industry is going and the market in general is going is just really fascinating, but it's nowhere near niche anymore.

Coffee has become a broadly understood product and industry, which is fantastic. It's what everyone's been working on for the last sort of decade or so, in London. We've got down to the point now where it's the subject of a McDonald's advert, right? I think that's indicative of where it is as well to a degree.

Why is there a coffee program but no tea program?
Richard: You're absolutely right; it's fascinating. We've talked with one of the guys at Caffeine Magazine, a publication here in the U.K. and he's a big proponent of the specialty roasters and has been heavily involved in the U.K. specialty coffee scene over the last decade. He's just a lovely guy, who has been championing exactly that. He's trying to get people to go down the tea rabbit hole, because it's still relatively untouched. We work with Postcard Tea across all of our bars. But it hasn't got the same appeal at the moment. I think it might come down to the fact that we're so familiar with it as a product. Coffee has been introduced to us in the way that it exists now relatively recently. But everyone in the U.K. has an opinion on tea and an expectation. It's almost harder to break that down.

—

Left: Claridge's Hotel. Right: Richard Frazier

Common Ground

WORDS Elyssa Goldberg, Melanie Marti
PHOTOGRAPHS Adam Goldberg, Daniela Velasco

The frantic life of a city-dweller can contribute to a reputation of indifference among Londoners. But you would never know this from walking into one of the major specialty coffee shops in the city. These coffee shops have inhaled the infectious energy of London and exhaled exactly what Londoners require from them—quality, efficiency, and, most importantly, community. The independent nature of these shops allows them to connect customers with quality coffee on a more personal basis, an asset in a city as big as London.

James Hennebry & Mat Russell, Rosslyn

Monmouth Coffee Copmany

ROSSLYN

According to James Hennebry, co-owner of Rosslyn Coffee, Londoner's attitudes toward coffee are changing: "People are a lot more discerning these days. Coffee is moving away from being a commodity product." He compared it to Melbourne—using his experience at Five Senses Coffee in Melbourne and later at Caravan Coffee Roasters in London as a baseline. In Melbourne, strong cafe culture makes sure that the cafe and the coffee are highlighted in equal measure; London, which has long had strong cafe culture, is just now incorporating high-end coffee into the experience.

But high-end coffee does not mean sacrificing approachability. As a Friedhats Kenyan coffee was placed into my hands, Hennebry noted, "Exceptional coffee doesn't have to be served up in an environment which is stuffy or exclusive." Rosslyn is neither of those things: The shop radiates sociability and inclusiveness, from the personable staff to the deliberate open design of the space.

Hennebry and the staff at Rosslyn are truly proud of the connections they make with their vendors and customers—and it shows. The guest coffees are carefully chosen and outwardly promoted. Latte art champions pour milk steadily into millennial pink ceramic mugs specially made for the shop. The minimal seating is done purposely to create a natural flow through the cafe, catering to the needs of its customers by providing efficiency. Every element of Rosslyn is customer-oriented. It's what makes Rosslyn one of the best new cafes in the world.

MONMOUTH COFFEE COMPANY

Situated in the outer edges of North London, a small, family-run shop called Claude W Dennis serves Monmouth coffee. The beans, which they buy wholesale, fuel live music shows and espresso martini nights at the shop.

Monmouth has been a strong, steady current running through London's coffee scene since 1978, when it became what some consider to be the city's first specialty roaster. Roasting and retailing coffee first in Covent Garden and then at a second location in Bermondsey, Monmouth has been purchasing beans from small lots and single farms, estates, and cooperatives maintaining its street cred long after the rise of Costa, Peet's, and Starbucks. When the crowds clear up, the staff remains focused as ever on spreading the good word—they'll tell you why they only serve full fat milk (it tastes better) and everything you've ever wanted to know about coffee origins—without the didactic approach of some of
its contemporaries.

WORKSHOP COFFEE

Another key player in the London coffee scene is Workshop Coffee. Find a seat next to countless laptops at the Old Street branch, which provides communal tables with seating for up to 40 people in a large converted factory. The out-of-office workspace is in equal measure for a recluse as it is for those hoping for a social vibe without a coworking membership. The cavernous, 1,300 sq. ft. room, which has exposed ducts and pipes, is simple, but it allows great coffee to speak for itself. Convoluted coffee talk is for other shops, but not for Workshop (though they'll certainly explain every detail of the coffee if you ask). Here, you'll find easy-to-follow, step-by-step brewing guides to take home (also available online). As with many of the major players in London, Workshop is for anyone, and community is valued above all else.

OZONE COFFEE ROASTERS

Ambition and attention to detail just barely begin to express what happens at Ozone Coffee, which opened its first location in 1998 in the small, New Zealand surf town of New Plymouth, and crossed many ponds to eventually open locations in Clerkenwell, Shoreditch, and Spitalfields in London starting in 2012. Years later, Ozone is best-known for its Kiwi approach to cafes, beautifully blurring the line between restaurant and coffee shop, as rabbit ragu and gem lettuces with citrus-cured mackerel occupy the same strata of importance as what's on the bar. These are places where each coffee drink—filter, espresso, latte, and so on—comes paired with specific bean blends. It even recently required Has Bean Coffee, based out of Stafford, England for its expertise in green bean sourcing and online sales. Which is all to say: Ozone is an empire, and the hordes of Silicon Roundabout workers hosting spontaneous meetings or refueling while hunched over laptops are its faithful subjects.

—

Ozone Coffee Roasters LONDON 141

Cinnamon Roll, Ozone Coffee Roasters

Smoked Fish Kedgeree with Poached Egg, Fried Shallots, Labneh & Chimichurri, Ozone Coffee Roasters

Seeeded Granola with Spiced Quince & Burnt Honey Labneh, Ozone Coffee Roasters

One at a Time:
Q&A with Russell Stradmoor

INTERVIEW Adam Goldberg
PHOTOGRAPHS Daniela Velasco

It takes 12, long hours to reach Tokyo from London by plane. Not that you would ever know once you step inside Omotesando Koffee in the Fitzrovia neighborhood of London. The cafe performs a miraculous feat of teleportation in seconds.

Omotesando Koffee—the "K" representing coffee through the lens of Kunitomo—welcomes guests to a universe of perfect geometric symmetry, where exacting baristas pour coffee from inside of a lab-like blond-wood cube. The precision and seriousness of the place are balanced with that signature brand of Japanese hospitality—impeccable attention to detail yet welcoming and serene.

Named for a posh Tokyo neighborhood, Omotesando Koffee has been redefining the idea of the minimalist cafe oasis since it first opened in a quiet Japanese back alley in 2011. Since then, founder Eiichi Kunitomo and his business partner Russell Stradmoor have brought their sensibility for coffee and design to cities all over Asia, from Singapore to Hong Kong to Bangkok. And, now, London? Here, Russell Stradmoor discusses why they chose London, how Omotesando Koffee is approaching its first foray into Europe, and how they are planning for world domination one cube at a time.

Damiano Archetti, Omotesando Koffee

Why did you choose London? I'm actually a quarter English on my father's side and I've always enjoyed visiting London over the years. Growing up, I've just built an affinity toward the city and its people. It was also important for Omotesando Koffee to branch further, having opened several successful locations throughout Asia. We wanted to test ourselves in a different type of city full of culture and coffee fanatics. Some people back home felt uneasy about us going to Europe, as there are so many coffee heavyweights and legendary coffee brands here. However, I just felt like it was time for London to experience something new and slightly different coffee-wise.

What does the square throughout the branding signify? When creating the cube, Kunitomo took inspiration from the traditional Japanese tea ceremony, where one serves another in a close and intimate setting on a square *tatami* mat. He felt that, when serving his customers, the barista and customer should connect not only through coffee but also on a personal level. The cube also acts as a platform, a stage, for the barista to perform and serve. Kunitomo didn't like the idea of working behind another traditional, long coffee bar, where the barista hides behind the machinery. Baristas should be proud of their coffee and proud to showcase their work.

How important is design when drinking coffee at a coffee shop? Design and aesthetics are very important to Omotesando Koffee. Many places serve good coffee, but they don't necessarily have the best atmosphere. We try and create the best experience for our customers through our coffee, design, and hospitality. We want to offer the most minimalistic, serene setting, so that our customers can focus and enjoy the coffee and its brewing process. Everything in our space serves a purpose and is meticulously thought through. For example, the height of our coffee counter is raised nearly two inches in London versus Asia; as our research shows, the average Londoner is 1.8 inches taller than the average Japanese customer. Many times, when people design a space, it's about what they can add to "upgrade" the experience. For us, it's about trimming down in order to further refine the space.

Tell us about the square canelés offered at all locations. Why are they the only food option? We call them *kashi* and, in my opinion, they taste better than most French canelés. In Japanese, *okashi* means sweets, so we simply refer to them as *kashi*. We've been serving them since day one and they go great with our espresso. We've been meaning to expand our food offerings in London, like we do in most other locations, but the coffee side has just been super busy. Having said that, we are working tirelessly to ensure new food items come out over the next few weeks. It's important that the food is executed at a very high level and complements the coffee.

What makes Omotesando Koffee Japanese? While the brand originates from Japan and its founder is Japanese, Omotesando Koffee has evolved over the years. Having said that, we focus and strive to keep many of its Japanese elements, such as the service, the style, and the attention to detail shown throughout the space. We stay true to our philosophy and would never compromise our quality for the sake of profit or convenience.

How would you describe your philosophy? We keep the sense of *omotenashi*. *Omotenashi* is hard to define, but it's the Japanese approach to service and hospitality. From customer interaction and atmosphere to the level of precision and staying true to one's craft—this is all part of omotenashi. Omotesando Koffee, since its humble beginnings in 2011, is still very much Japanese through and through.

Where do you think London coffee scene is in comparison to Tokyo or Hong Kong? Both are highly developed markets, but London is extremely different in its direction and evolution. Regarding roasters, Japan has an abundance of small, relatively unknown, but niche, high-quality roasters, such as Unlimited Coffee and Bontain Coffee. The U.K. has large roasters such as Assembly, Square Mile, and Ozone. Hand-drip coffee culture is very popular in Japan while milk-based coffees are preferred in London. The direction of espresso also varies in both cities. While Londoners mostly prefer strong and bold flavours, the Japanese palate is much more sensitive.

Did you have to adjust any recipes or menu offerings for your London opening? We definitely had to adjust some recipes here in London. Kunitomo, our head of coffee Miki, and I first started coming to London to do our research eight months before our Fitzrovia opening in December of 2018. London was a big move for us, and it was important that we got things right. We needed to understand the Londoners' coffee palates, preferred flavor profiles, and ingredients—from the local milk down to the local water. The blend we serve here in London is roasted by Assembly Coffee, and they are awesome. It took several months for us and Assembly to get the blend just right, mainly due to the finer details and the difficulties of continued testing between London and Tokyo. Nick Mabey, who is head of product at Assembly, said it was probably the most unique and precise process he's worked on. In the end, we were all very happy with the final product.

What's next? World domination? That's a joke, but who knows? If you told me two years ago that we'd open a beautiful shop in Central London, I would have laughed in disbelief. This year, we open our two new flagships in Tokyo's Kiyosumi-Shirakawa district and Hong Kong's brand new K11 Musea in July and September, respectively. The new space in Hong Kong will feature our sister brand KOFFEE MAMEYA, which will be our first one of those outside of Japan. The journey continues and who knows where it will take us. One coffee at a time.

—

APPENDIX

London:

AIDA
133 Shoreditch High St,
London E1 6JE, UK

Allpress Espresso
58 Redchurch St,
London E2 7DP, UK

Allpress Espresso (Roastery)
55 Dalston Ln,
London E8 2NG, UK

artFix
51 Powis St, Woolwich,
London SE18 6HZ, UK

Assembly Coffee
244 Ferndale Rd, Brixton,
London SW9 8FR, UK

Benk & Bo.
4-6 Gravel Ln, Spitalfields,
London E1 7AW, UK

Boxpark Shoreditch
2-10 Bethnal Green Rd,
London E1 6GY, UK

Café 1001
91 Brick Ln,
London E1 6QL, UK

Caravan Coffee Roasters
11-13 Exmouth Market
London, EC1R 4Qd, UK

Caravan Coffee Roasters
152 Great Portland Street
London, W1W 6AJ, UK

Caravan Coffee Roasters
1 Granary Square
London N1C 4AA, UK

Caravan Coffee Roasters
22 Bloomberg Arcade
London, EC4N 8AR, UK

Caravan Coffee Roasters
30 Great Guildford Street
London SE1 0HS, Uk

Claridge's
Brook St, Mayfair,
London W1K 4HR, UK

Claud W Dennis Coffee
3 Chase Side,
London N14 5PB, UK

Climpson & Sons Coffee
67 Broadway Market,
London E8 4PH, UK

Coffee Junction
42 Provost St, Hoxton,
London N1 7SU, UK

Daylesford Organic
208-212 Westbourne Grove,
London W11 2RH, UK

Daylesford Organic
44B Pimlico Rd, Belgravia,
London SW1W 8LP, UK

Daylesford Organic
6-8 Blandford St, Marylebone,
London W1U 4AU, UK

Department of Coffee and Social Affairs
3 Lowndes Ct, Soho,
London W1F 7HD, UK

Fin & Flounder
71 Broadway Market,
London E8 4PH, UK

Fix 126
126 Curtain Rd,
London EC2A 3PJ, UK

Giro Cycles
2 High St,
Esher KT10 9RT, UK

Glitterati
842-844 Green Lanes, Winchmore Hill,
London N21 2RT, UK

Honeypie Bakery
Marylebone Farmers Market, Aybrook St,
Marylebone, London W1U 4DF, UK

H.R. Higgins
79 Duke St, Mayfair,
London W1K 5AS, UK

KANA London
5A Gransden Ave,
London E8 3QA, UK

Lily Vanilli Bakery
6, The Courtyard, Ezra St,
London E2 7RH, UK

Madame Gautier
4 Enterprise Way, White City,
London NW10 6UG, UK

Marylebone Farmers Market
Aybrook St, Marylebone,
London W1U 4DF, UK

Mason & Painter
67 Columbia Rd,
London E2 7RG, UK

Milagros
61 Columbia Rd,
London E2 7RG, UK

Monmouth
2 Park St,
London SE1 9AB, UK

Monmouth
27 Monmouth St,
London WC2H 9EU, UK

Mouse Tail Coffee Stories
307 Whitechapel Rd,
London E1 1BY, UK

New North Cofee
Jubilee House, 197-213 Oxford St, Soho,
London W1D 2LF, UK

Omotesando Koffee
Fitzrovia,
London W1J 5EZ, UK

Origin Coffee Roasters
65 Charlotte Rd,
London EC2A 3PE, UK

Origin Coffee Roasters
96 Euston Rd,
London NW1 2DB, UK

Origin Coffee Roasters
The Aircraft Factory, 100 Cambridge
Grove, London W6 0LE, UK

Ozone Coffee Roasters
11 Leonard St,
London EC2A 4AQ, UK

Pact Coffee Pop Up
45 Brushfield St,
London E1 6AA, UK

Paper & Cup
18, Calvert Ave,
London E2 7JP, United Kingdom

Pavilion Bakery
18 Broadway Market,
London E8 4QJ, UK

APPENDIX

Pavilion Bakery
130 Columbia Rd,
London E2 7RG, UK

Printers & Stationers
21A Ezra St,
London E2 7RH, UK

Prufrock Coffee
23-25 Leather Ln,
London EC1N 7TE, UK

Rapha Cycling Club
85 Brewer St, Soho,
London W1F 9ZN, UK

Rotate
Unit 6, durham yard, 5 Teesdale St,
London E2 6QF, UK

Rosslyn Coffee
78 Queen Victoria St,
London EC4N 4SJ, UK

Sawmill Cafe
51-53 W Ham Ln,
London E15 4PH, UK

SkandiHus
90 De Beauvoir Rd,
London N1 4EN, UK

Square Mile Coffee Roasters
Unit 13 Uplands Business Park,
Blackhorse Ln, London E17 5QJ, UK

Steve Edge Design
2 Hoxton St,
London N1 6NG, UK

Strongroom Bar and Kitchen
120-124 Curtain Rd, Shoreditch,
London EC2A 3SQ, UK

The Ace Hotel
100 Shoreditch High St,
London E1 6JQ, UK

The Attendant
27A Foley St, Fitzrovia,
London W1W 6DY, UK

The Attendant
74 Great Eastern St,
London EC2A 3JL, UK

The Attendant
75 Leather Ln,
London EC1N 7TJ, UK

The Frenchie
16 Henrietta St, Covent Garden,
London WC2E 8QH, UK

The Grand Howl
214 Well St,
London E9 6QT, UK

The London School of Coffee
3a, Imperial studios, Imperial Rd,
Fulham, London SW6 2AG, UK

The Pilgrim Hotel
25 London St, Paddington,
London W2 1HH, UK

The Roastery at Tate
Tate Britain, Millbank, Westminster,
London SW1P 4RG, UK

The Truman Brewery
91 Brick Ln,
London E1 6QR, UK

Turning Earth
Railway Arches, 361-362 Whiston Rd,
London E2 8BW, UK

Workshop Coffee
1 Barrett St, Marylebone,
London W1U 1AX, UK

Workshop Coffee
60 Holborn Viaduct,
London EC1A 2FD, UK

Workshop Coffee
7AD, 1 Old St,
London, UK

Workshop Coffee
80 Mortimer St, Marylebone,
London W1W 7FE, UK

Workshop Coffee (Roastery)
29-43 Vyner St,
London E2 9DQ, UK

Vintage Heaven
82 Columbia Rd,
London E2 7QB, UK

International Locations:

Boutique Coffee
327 E 4th Ave,
San Mateo, CA 94401

Five Senses Coffee
300 Rosslyn St,
Melbourne VIC 3003, Australia

Menta Specialty Coffee Shop
9A, Florinis, Nicosia,
Lefkosa, Cyprus

Sage & Sirloin
Wali Al Ahd Hwy,
Hamala, Bahrain

**
This list represents coffee shops visited, referenced, or interviewed on background for the making of Drift, Volume 8: London.

London

instagram/@driftmag
twitter/@driftny
facebook/driftny

www.driftmag.com